Economic terms in the news during the Great Recession

Linguistic Insights

Studies in Language and Communication

Edited by Maurizio Gotti,
Emeritus Professor,
University of Bergamo (Italy).

Volume 303

ADVISORY BOARD
Vijay Bhatia (Hong Kong)
David Crystal (Bangor)
Konrad Ehlich (Berlin / München)
Jan Engberg (Aarhus)
Norman Fairclough (Lancaster)
John Flowerdew (Hong Kong)
Ken Hyland (East Anglia)
Roger Lass (Cape Town)
Françoise Salager-Meyer (Mérida, Venezuela)
Srikant Sarangi (Cardiff)
Susan Šarčević (Rijeka)
Lawrence Solan (New York)

Javier Fernández-Cruz / Antonio Moreno-Ortiz

Economic terms in the news during the Great Recession

A diachronic sentiment and collocational analysis

PETER LANG

Lausanne - Berlin - Bruxelles - Chennai - New York - Oxford

Bibliographic information published by die Deutsche Nationalbibliothek
Die Deutsche Nationalbibliothek lists this publication in the Deutsche National-bibliografie; detailed bibliographic data is available on the Internet at ‹http://dnb.d-nb.de›.

Library of Congress Cataloging-in-Publication Data
A CIP catalog record for this book has been applied for at the Library of Congress.

This book was published thanks to:
Project "Linguistically-motivated Sentiment Analysis with Rhetorical and Discourse Parsing (DisParSA)", financed by the 2020 Research, Development and Innovation Fund of the Spanish Ministry of Science and Innovation (PID2020-115310RB-I00).
A Margarita Salas research fellowship supported by the Spanish Ministry of Universities and financed within the Next Generation EU funds.

ISSN 1424-8689
E-ISBN 978-3-0343-4781-5 (E-PDF)
DOI 10.3726/b21287

ISBN 978-3-0343-4778-5 (Print)
E-ISBN 978-3-0343-4782-2 (E-PUB)

© 2024 Peter Lang Group AG, Lausanne
Published by
Peter Lang Group AG, Lausanne, Switzerland

info@peterlang.com
http://www.peterlang.com/

All rights reserved.
All parts of this publication are protected by copyright.
Any utilisation outside the strict limits of the copyright law, without the permission of the publisher, is forbidden and liable to prosecution. This applies in particular to reproductions, translations, microfilming, and storage and processing in electronic retrieval systems.

Table of Contents

1 Introduction 9

2 Research design 15
   2.1 Research questions and objectives 15
   2.2 Corpus 16
   2.3 Method 16
   2.4 Instruments 20
      2.4.1 Sentiment analysis software 20
      2.4.2 Corpus statistics tools 23

3 The influence of the economy and the press on language 25
   3.1 Online content and opinion 31

4 Evaluative language 35
   4.1 Terms and concepts in evaluative language 37
   4.2 Definition of evaluation 41
   4.3 Functions of evaluation 43
   4.4 Markers of evaluation 45
   4.5 Evaluation in journalistic genres 48

5 Formal models for the study of evaluative language 51
   5.1 Liu's model 51
   5.2 Benamara's model 55

6 Sentiment analysis 59
   6.1 Definition and applications 59
   6.2 Classification levels 63
      6.2.1 Document-level sentiment classification 63
      6.2.2 Sentence-level sentiment classification 64
      6.2.3 Aspect-level sentiment classification 66
   6.3 Machine learning approaches to sentiment analysis 69
   6.4 Lexicon-based sentiment analysis 72

		6.4.1 Sentiment lexicon generation 73

      6.4.1 Sentiment lexicon generation 73
      6.4.2 Available sentiment lexicons 74
      6.4.3 Contextual valence shifters 76
  6.5 Domain-specific sentiment classification 78
      6.5.1 Economics and sentiment analysis 80
      6.5.2 Characteristics of the economic-financial domain in relation to sentiment analysis 82
      6.5.3 Economic sentiment dictionaries 84

7 Language change and semantic prosody 87
  7.1 Semantic change, sentiment, and *event words* 89
  7.2 Semantic prosody 90

8 Data analysis 93
  8.1 Term 1: 'credit' 94
      8.1.1 Sentiment analysis 94
      8.1.2 Usage fluctuation analysis 97
            8.1.2.1 First phase (2007) 97
            8.1.2.2 Second phase (2008–2012) 98
            8.1.2.3 Third phase (2013–2015) 102
  8.2 Term 2: 'debt' 104
      8.2.1 Sentiment analysis 105
      8.2.2 Usage fluctuation analysis 108
            8.2.2.1 First phase (2007) 108
            8.2.2.2 Second phase (2008–2011) 110
            8.2.2.3 Third phase (2012–2015) 115
  8.3 Term 3: 'markets' 118
      8.3.1 Sentiment analysis 119
      8.3.2 Usage fluctuation analysis 122
            8.3.2.1 First phase (2007) 122
            8.3.2.2 Second phase (2008–2011) 124
            8.3.2.3 Third phase (2012–2014) 126
            8.3.2.4 Fourth phase (2015) 127
  8.4 Term 4: 'housing' 130
      8.4.1 Sentiment analysis 130
      8.4.2 Usage fluctuation analysis 133
            8.4.2.1 First phase (2007–2012) 133
            8.4.2.2 Second phase (2013–2015) 136

Table of Contents

9 Discussion and conclusions 141

List of Figures 147

List of Tables 149

References 151

1 Introduction

It can hardly be contested that the economy is one of the leading factors of social change, if not the top one, as it is a powerful driver that determines the lives of individuals around the world, as well as geopolitical entities, societies, and, ultimately, the world. Global macroeconomic events, therefore, have a profound impact on all aspects of society, including language. An economic crisis, for example, is likely to spark off a number of crucial changes in the living conditions of millions of people worldwide, but it also has the potential to shape human languages, as they adapt to describe the new situation. In this regard, the role of the media, and their potential to shape people's ideas, should not be underestimated. During times of crisis, specialized news outlets act as an oracle that explains and interprets ongoing events, and attempts to predict future developments and outcomes. Needless to say, they primarily use language to accomplish their communication objectives and, whether consciously or not, they choose to use certain words and expressions over others. What is relevant from a purely linguistic point of view is that these lexical choices may eventually result in subtle (and sometimes not so subtle) changes in the semantics of words over a relatively short period of time, as they are used to express – and sometimes impose – a particular worldview, if not to manipulate trends and markets.

The purpose of this book is to explore how the meaning of specialized terms used to describe key macroeconomic indicators can experience significant shifts in connotation during major economic events, as reflected in their usage in mass media. From a sentiment analysis perspective, the book seeks to provide a detailed analysis of how such changes in connotation may occur and what factors may influence them, drawing on a range of case studies and examples from the Great Recession. By shedding light on the complex relationship between language, media, and macroeconomic phenomena, this book aims to contribute to a deeper understanding of the role that language plays in shaping our perceptions and responses to economic events.

Entering the term 'rescue' in a search engine in the early summer of 2019 would primarily return news about aids to US producers in the midst of a trade war with China. A year earlier, results would be about the NGO Open Arms and the rescue of human beings off the coast of Libya during the dramatic migration crisis in the Mediterranean. In 2008, we would most likely get results about the collapse of the global banking system asking to be 'bailed out' by states.

Beyond being a dark analogy, this example serves to illustrate the profound subjective nature of the texts that we find when we open a newspaper. Importantly, the sentiment that the word 'rescue' evokes in each case is very different. Thus the question arises: is communication and, consequently, the terminology used in it an instrument for subliminally projecting the sentiment of economic policies whose potential we are but beginning to glimpse? Specialized languages have their own terminology, expressions and constructions, which are far from unchanging, and which also reflect the spirit of the times. All these factors come to light in the way in which evaluations and opinions are expressed in texts.

Fifteen years after the events of 2008, the world is witnessing new and difficult challenges to the economy, but still has not forgotten – and is still suffering the consequences of – the effects of the Great Recession. On August 9, 2008 the European Central Bank and the US Federal Reserve had to intervene to tackle a banking system that had come to a grinding halt by injecting 100 billion euros. It was the day that 'changed the world', according to Adam Appelgarth, then head of the British bank Northern Rock and one of the 'twenty-five faces of the economic disaster', as published by the British newspaper The Guardian (Finch/Clark/Teather 2009). From that summer onwards, wholesale market activity began to plummet and months later the most iconic event of the Great Recession took place: on September 15, 2008, the US investment bank Lehman Brothers went bankrupt, thus initiating a global episode that a decade later continues to have repercussions on our daily lives. Although there was no bailout for Lehman, it was the first time that the public became aware of the term 'bailout' in an economic context, and it connoted, rather than a threshold of hope, a halo of concern.

That autumn was key in political, economic and, of course, linguistic terms. In the three weeks following the collapse of Lehman Brothers, the financial markets panicked and it was the first time that the public heard terms hitherto used exclusively in technical jargon, for example, the paradigmatic 'credit crunch', a term that initially referred to private banks refusing to give each other loans and that ended up spreading as a metonymy for that stage of the crisis. Since then, words such as 'credit' or 'debt' have become part of all forums and discussions, and have acquired different connotations depending on the economic context.

Governments promised to save the system by reinforcing both the banking sector and the public and private economy. Faced with the seriousness of a situation which was not yet fully evident to the population, a scenario of discursive action took place, more performative than philosophical: the main actors at the global level, such as Nicolas Sarkozy, pronounced themselves on a capitalist system that had run amok and had become an outdated entity that had to be restated on the basis of work and morality (Sarkozy 2008). In Spain, Rodríguez Zapatero's cabinet decided to use euphemisms such as 'desaceleración acelerada', 'dificultad que nos viene de fuera' and 'ajuste duro' ('accelerated deceleration', 'some difficulties coming from outside', 'hard adjustment', respectively) in order to avoid the use of any direct reference to the explosion of the crisis (Garea 2008). These examples illustrate the power that the Great Recession had to spur changes in political discourse, which is in turn immediately reflected in the press and, consequently, provokes perlocutionary reactions among the different social actors, including the general population.

In the social sphere, new citizen movements flourished on a global scale around 2011 in response to the paradigm shift brought about by the crisis. These gained considerable traction and unheard-of social relevance, to the point that protesters were recognized as Time magazine's figure of the year. The discursive shift provoked by citizen social actors such as the 15-M Movement in Spain, the overflow of traditional trade unionism in Greece, or the Occupy Wall Street protest camps initially in the United States and subsequently expanded to the rest of the world, opened a breach for new citizen-driven debates that questioned the 'official' experts' discourse in the context of economic austerity policies.

Citizen participation in the political discourse meant an exponential acceleration in the exchange of transformative ideas, as the debate permeated deeply into all strata of society and, as a consequence, had profound political repercussions. From an eminently informative translation of political and economic decisions, some of the consequences of the austerity policies acquired a human face, such as the drama of evictions, or the consequences of funding cuts in public services.

Institutionally, the impact of these movements ultimately triggered the end of the two-party system in Spain, following the emergence of new political actors on both sides of the left-right political axis. In the rest of the world, some traditionally minority political representations were pushed forward, as illustrated by the ascent of Alexis Tsipras to the Greek government or the emergence of new figures in the Anglo world, such as the leadership of Jeremy Corbyn in the British Labour Party, or the meteoric candidacy of Bernie Sanders in the Democratic Party, both with eminently popular support outside the impetus of lobbies and other traditional interest groups.

Another consequence is the rise of right-wing populism in several countries around the world, including the United States and the United Kingdom. In the US, the election of Donald Trump in 2016 represented a major shift towards right-wing populist politics, with his rhetoric and policies emphasizing protectionism, anti-immigration sentiment, and a rejection of political correctness. Similarly, the 2016 Brexit referendum in the UK was driven in part by populist rhetoric, with the *Leave* campaign arguing for the control of the British economy, which was allegedly in the hands of the European Union. Other countries, such as Hungary and Poland, have also seen the rise of right-wing populist movements, often characterized by a focus on national identity, authoritarianism, and a rejection of liberal democratic norms. These movements have tapped into fears and frustrations among segments of the population who feel left behind by globalization and threatened by demographic change.

The popularization of a number of specialized discursive elements develops, among other factors, due to the need to describe the unfolding events of the crisis. At the same time, online press and social networks gained traction, to the detriment of traditional media, whose discursive development was accompanied by a sharp turn in economic, social and political factors. For the last two decades, Internet access has become virtually universal: dynamic websites and social networks are now at the core of a hyperconnected world that has far-reaching impact on people's lives, especially when compared to that of traditional mass media. Today, the Internet is a multidirectional space for socialization and exchange of opinions, a global agora where debates arise among users from all over the world. As a result, information, and with it new uses of language, is nowadays disseminated not only by the press and traditional media, but also by the voice of the public on social networks.

Traditional mass media, on the other hand, continue to set the tone for public opinion, since the resources are concentrated in the hands of a few private conglomerates and, during an economic crisis, their formative function is made more apparent, as they need to explain the basic terms and concepts of a specialized domain – economics – to the general public, to provide an interpretation of the political-economic situation, and to serve as a watchtower to observe opinion in street-level debates. Thus, online general newspapers are, given their mediating role, one of the best reflections of the discourse of an era, and act as a proxy source for truthful information of language in use (Gouws et al. 2011; Toret Medina 2015).

2 Research design

2.1 Research questions and objectives

The following research questions have driven our work:

- Does the semantic orientation or connotations of terms change as the words they associate with (i.e., co-occur with) change their polarity?
- Do higher-order historical events, such as crises, drive rapid changes in the semantic orientation of terms?

Our research takes three main methodological assumptions. First, language is a highly dynamic system that reflects the evolution of the subjective connotations, attitudes, evaluations and stance of words used on a daily basis. Second, there are significant short-term sentiment changes in economic terms once they become event words. Finally, these changes can be tracked by looking at the contexts in which they occur.

Thus, our main aim is to analyze the fluctuations in the semantic orientation of selected economic terms within the period 2007–2015 and offer a description of the impact of higher order events on those semantic variations. Then, for these terms, we aim to identify the factors (social, political, economic, etc.) that have accompanied changes in usage, from a sentiment perspective, during the period 2007–2015. Finally, we will attempt to identify possible variations in the semantic prosody of the terms under study over the years.

2.2 Corpus

In order to achieve these objectives, our main data source is the *Great Recession News Corpus* (GRNC) (Fernández-Cruz/Moreno-Ortiz 2020), a specialized corpus in the economic/financial domain that comprises approximately 35,000 articles from the business sections of *The Guardian* (52.9 %) and *The New York Times* (47.1 %) published between 2007 and 2015. Its latest version contains approximately 26 million words. *The Guardian* and *The New York Times* are considered to be among the top influential newspapers in the world (comScore 2012). Ideologically, they are usually placed in the centre-left spectrum. The resulting corpus includes 31 million tokens, which meets the classic requirements in corpus linguistics (e.g., McEnery/Xiao/Tono 2006): electronic, size, authenticity, and specific criteria.

2.3 Method

The methodology consists in analyzing the contexts (sentences) in which the selected terms occur using a number of methods, which we describe below. The criteria for the selection of the terms in this study were, strictly speaking, based on intuition, but taking into account their status as keywords in the corpus, as well as the historical and economic context. The chosen terms for this study are 'credit', 'debt', 'housing', and 'markets'. These four words, while belonging in the specialized domain of finance and economics, have transcended to the general public and become commonplace in general language in English (and their equivalents in other languages). Table 1.1 shows the counts for each focus word by year.

Table 1.1 Number of sentences extracted for each focus term

Year	credit	debt	markets	housing	Total
2007	577	392	628	290	1,597
2008	1,214	706	1,259	459	3,179
2009	980	949	761	252	2,690
2010	942	1,139	1,081	300	3,162
2011	1,043	1,869	1,845	351	4,757
2012	948	2,270	2,015	330	5,233
2013	975	1,251	1,851	594	4,077
2014	992	1,314	2,166	732	4,472
2015	990	2,066	2,762	671	5,818
Total	8,661	11,956	14,368	3,979	34,985

Thus, in this book we present a longitudinal, corpus-based study whose ultimate goal is to detect and analyze variations in sentiment of a set of terms from the economic-financial domain that acquired public relevance during the crisis. Longitudinal research is a loose set of methods that share one thing in common: data is collected around targets over a series of time points. The longitudinal model is often used in mixed models, as it requires qualitative insights related to the statistical trends observed.

The objectives of longitudinal studies have two main purposes: to describe patterns of change and to explain causal relationships. In this book we propose to describe changes in sentiment in specialized words and to explain these changes through their relationship to crisis-related socio-political events. In this case, we speak of longitudinal cross-sectional or trend studies that analyze changes over time within a given population simply through repeated sampling over time.

We study sentiment through the time series in order to look for patterns of change in individual cases, and identify them across time periods. Modelling the dynamics of public opinion through time series can be achieved by aggregating data points for each of the time periods considered – in our case we will use the text sentiment score (TSS) that our sentiment analysis tool, Lingmotif, calculates. The nature and number of texts will depend in each case on the specific dynamics to be addressed. The difference between correctly identifying a model or not lies mainly in identifying the different concurrent phenomena in the time series, as well as identifying each of its structural changes and their nature (Fernández-Cruz/Baixauli-Pérez 2018).

The evolution of the sentiment associated with terms, just like the study of any natural dynamic system, is potentially influenced by a wide variety of external variables, which will cause structural changes of different types, magnitude, position and duration. In order to observe the evolution of the semantic orientation of each of the contexts of our focus terms over the time series, the following process was carried out:

1. From the GRNC, all sentences in which the focus terms occurred were extracted and four datasets were created, one for each term.
2. These datasets were analyzed with Lingmotif plus the domain-specific *plug-in* lexicon *SentiEcon*. This returned a Text Sentiment Score (TSS) for each sentence in the range 0 (extremely negative) to 100 (extremely positive).
3. For each term, a statistical analysis was performed using the Pandas library of the Python programming language and the Lancaster Stats Tools (Brezina 2018). The total sentiment scores were statistically aggregated by using yearly averages. In this way, the yearly variation of the sentiment scores of the context of each term under study could be observed without seasonality. We perform annual parametric (one-way ANOVA, post-hoc tests: Bonferroni adjusted t-test, p-values) and non-parametric (Kruskal/Wallis 1952) statistical analyses with the Lancaster Stats Tools online. The hypotheses are as follows: (a) $H_0: \mu_1 = \mu_2 = \mu_3 \ldots = \mu_9$, and (b) H_1: means are not all equal.
4. In order to observe general trends in a more detailed manner, we aggregate the TSS figures by quarterly averages and calculate the relative frequency of the terms for each of the 36 data points (four quarters, nine years) of the time series. To smooth out noise and seasonality, we plotted general sentiment trends using a regression model (Linear GAM) of sentiment scores on a regression curve with 95 % and 99 % confidence intervals (Wood 2017). The dispersion points are fitted and analyzed using the peaks-and-troughs[1] (Gabrielatos et al.

---

1 'Peaks-and-troughs' is a technique used in time series of diverse nature to identify trends in data by analyzing the high (peaks) and low (troughs) points of a chart over a certain period of time.

2012) technique, which we use to measure the difference in sentiment/frequency between consecutive points during the period.
5. We apply Usage Fluctuation Analysis (UFA) (McEnery/Brezina/Baker 2022) implemented in the Lancaster Stat Tools[2] to the dataset of collocations by year, which provides a concise and reliable comparison through a specific timeline. The parameters used in the tool were as follows: Window= 2, cut-off logDice > 7, Latency Threshold = 3, Consistency Threshold = 80 %, 2 sampling points.
6. A limited set of representative collocations for each focus term were selected for qualitative analysis by examining concordance lines to provide a more detailed picture of how the focus terms are characterized over the time series.

The logDice coefficient was selected as a statistical indicator of collocation because it marks not only the frequency but also the exclusivity of collocation between the two lexical units. logDice is a standardized measure (in the range 0–14) which, unlike other measures such as T-Score or MI, avoids the bias produced by the size of the corpus. In this way, it is possible to compare the scores between results obtained in different annual subcorpora that have very different sizes (Gablasova/Brezina/McEnery 2017). In addition to providing better transparency and replicability values, it allowed validating the data by triangulating quantitative and qualitative results in order to establish relationships between the data and historical events.

In agreement with Neale/Flowerdew (2003), we believe that implementing this mixed methodological design allows us to benefit from the strengths and reduce the weaknesses of longitudinal experimental designs, so as to run a model that combines and complements extensive and intensive techniques. The extensive element refers to the quantitative analysis of sentiment (the descriptive, statistical work) and the intensive element that refers to the qualitative work directly related to the texts.

---

2 http://corpora.lancs.ac.uk/stats/toolbox.php

This triangulation refers to what Dörnyei (2007) calls 'validation by convergence' and allows us to ensure the validity of the research. If a finding endures a series of tests by different methods, it should be considered more valid than if a single method is used. In sum, this triangulation will allow us to delve deeper into the observation of the complex dynamics behind changes in the semantic orientation of specialized lexical units.

Longitudinal studies provide a good opportunity to observe the development of semantic orientation at the micro and macro levels. As a result, we expect to obtain clues indicating external historical motifs, as well as contextualizing narrative profiles related to such changes in semantic orientation. Throughout the analysis process we expect to identify trends and factors (changes in the economic situation, speeches, protests, changes in the political agenda, etc.) that are reflected in the news and caused changes in the semantic orientation of words.

2.4 Instruments

Although the tools and resources that we employ in this research are sufficiently described elsewhere, we provide here a minimal description of each of them to facilitate reading and to understand the basic functionalities they offer in relation to this particular study.

2.4.1 Sentiment analysis software

Lingmotif is a lexicon-based sentiment analysis system for Spanish and English developed by the Tecnolengua group at the University of Malaga whose original conceptualization dates back to 2010. Research in this field, initially dedicated to Spanish sentiment analysis, started with the Sentitext project (Moreno-Ortiz/Pérez Pozo/Torres Sánchez 2010) and after the launch of Lingmotif, an extensive English lexicon designed ad hoc together with a proprietary set of context rules was added. The system has been released in several presentations, first as a cross-platform desktop version for Windows,

MacOS and GNU-Linux developed in Python. The current version is offered as a client-server web application[3] with user and profiles management.

Lingmotif relies on a very large set of lexical sources and a database of context rules that are used together to detect textual segments that include sentiment, in order to generate a number of metrics that define the sentiment of a text. The Text Sentiment Score (TSS) qualifies a text according to its sentiment or polarity, while the Text Sentiment Intensity (TSI) provides a measure of the intensity of the text, with texts in lower end of the range being considered factual and scores at the upper end being highly evaluative (Moreno-Ortiz/Pérez-Hernández/Gómez-Pascual 2016). In summary, Lingmotif tokenizes the target text into its constituent sentences and subsequently detects and assigns a valence to the words and multiword expressions that include sentiment according to its data sources, taking into account contextual modifiers. For each language, the Lingmotif system contains a core lexicon, a set of context rules and, for domain-specific texts, optional, user-defined *plug-in* lexicons can be used that add new lexical items or override the valence of existing ones (Moreno-Ortiz/Pérez-Hernandez 2018). Lingmotif analyzes texts at the sentence level and calculates the overall score by weighing the number of positive and negative items and sentences.

The simple identification of lexical items as pertaining to a given semantic orientation is insufficient without the study of contextual factors as it can be intensified, attenuated, or inverted. Contextual valence shifters were first proposed by Polanyi/Zaenen (2006), but only two systems have actually implemented them: Lingmotif and SO-CAL (Taboada et al. 2011).

Lingmotif output consists of files in HTML, JSON, and CSV formats, and includes several kinds of metrics and word lists:

- Sentiment-related metrics and lists: TSS, TSI, positive, neutral and negative scores and lists of lexical items.
- Text metrics and statistics: number of tokens, types, sentences, type-token ratio, number of lexical and function words, number of single

---

3   https://ltl.uma.es/

and multi-words, number of items in each lexical word class, punctuation marks, and others.
- Social networks-specific statistics: number of hashtags, mentions, URLs, emojis.

Even though both Lingmotif's core lexicon and the SentiEcon plug-in lexicon have been evaluated with good results in the past, it is necessary to ascertain whether TSS classification with this particular dataset is accurate enough. Thus, we carried out a formal evaluation study using a random sample (n = 360) from the full set of sentences (N = 5,481) in our main dataset (Confidence Level = 95 %, Margin of Error = 5 %). Three annotators independently labeled the sample dataset as belonging in one of three classes (positive, negative, neutral). In order to avoid bias towards the lexicon-based classifier, annotators were asked to classify the sentences according to the overall sentiment they thought the sentences expressed, regardless of the number of sentiment words that were present in them. In order to ensure annotation reliability, Inter-Annotator Agreement (IAA) was calculated using the Disagree Python package (Price/Mensio 2022). Agreement was found to be very high for both Fleiss' kappa ($\kappa = 0.878$) and Krippendorff's alpha ($\alpha = 0.878$). The gold standard was arrived at by majority vote on differing labels, as no case was present where all three annotators disagreed on the label.

Precision and recall evaluation metrics were calculated using the scikit-learn (Pedregosa et al. 2011) Python library. With an overall accuracy of 76 % and a macro-averaged F1 score of 0.73, the classification predictions can be said to be quite acceptable for a multi-label classification task. The lowest scores were found to be for the neutral class, as Lingmotif's neutral classification can be arrived at in either of two very different ways: when no sentiment expression is found or when the positive and negative expressions cancel each other out. Table 1.2 shows the classification with all relevant evaluation metrics.

Instruments

Table 1.2 Lingmotif's evaluation metrics for three-way sentiment classification

	Precision	*Recall*	*F1-score*	*Support*
NEG	0.68	0.88	0.76	136
NEU	0.60	0.75	0.67	40
POS	0.92	0.67	0.77	184
Accuracy			0.76	360
Macro avg	0.73	0.76	0.73	360
Weighted avg	0.79	0.76	0.76	360

2.4.2 Corpus statistics tools

We rely on two corpus statistics tools: the Lancaster Stats Tools, and Sketch Engine (Kilgarriff et al. 2014), a well-known web-based corpus management and query suite that makes it easy to extract linguistic information and insights from large corpora in a very user-friendly, intuitive manner, including relative frequencies, keywords, collocations, and concordances.

The Lancaster Stats Tool is a more specialized tool that we employ to carry out Usage Fluctuation Analysis (UFA). This method attempts to examine the fluctuation of word usage manifested through collocation, that is, the co-occurrence of words in texts. The instrument calculates Gwet's AC1 agreement statistic, a measure of inter-annotator reliability that is used to assess the level of agreement between two or more annotators when assigning categorical ratings to a set of items.

McEnery et al. (2022), the original proponents of this method, use this statistical measure to calculate the agreement between different lists of collocates in a timeline. The technique relies on two simple assumptions: first, words co-occurring in the vicinity of other words provide insight into their usage (collocation principle) and, second, the change in the pattern of co-occurrence of words over time can identify points where their usage changes. The tool returns a set of collocation lists belonging in one of four categories:

- Consistent: collocates that do not change in the timeline.
- Initiating: collocates that emerge after the second data point and remain until the end of the series.

- Terminal: collocates that emerge in the last data points.
- Transient: collocates that emerge after the second data point and decline before the final data points.

Thus, this tool is of special interest to us, as it can help identify shifts in the sentiment of our focus terms by extracting collocational patterns that behave in specific ways over time.

Our data analysis is described in Chapter 8, but before we present it, it is necessary to develop the framework and theoretical tenets upon which it is based, which we do in the Chapters 3 to 7.

3 The influence of the economy and the press on language

The economic crisis that began in 2008 has been considered a testing ground for experimenting with all kinds of expressive resources to describe the nature of an extremely complicated economic situation. The bursting of the real estate bubble resulted in dire consequences for the living conditions of the population: prolonged unemployment, cutbacks in basic services and social assistance, as well as a housing crisis that involved hundreds of thousands of foreclosures and evictions. These events ushered in a new discursive era in which the use of economic language in discourse became ubiquitous. A paradigmatic case of this shift was Nicolas Sarkozy's call to refound capitalism (Luna-Alonso 2016) mentioned in Chapter 1.

The worsening of living conditions in large sectors of the population brought about drastic socio-political changes that put the spotlight on economic news and, consequently, on economic language. What is relevant to us is that such political and social reactions to austerity measures have influenced public discourse and, consequently, language. Thus, specialized financial terms that used to be used exclusively by experts quickly became widespread in general news and have been progressively adopted by the public (Holborow 2015).

Bednarek/Caple (2012) justify the study of economic discourse from journalistic texts giving three main reasons: (a) the abundance of texts of this type, (b) the ease to obtain them and, (c) the great public outreach, meaning that their message is likely to influence the linguistic community. The authors consider that news is shared and disseminated more than ever before in history, a situation in which social networks have played a key role. Thus, the media have more power than ever in history to influence and shape opinions, and so the use of language modifies ideas and beliefs, as well as the semantics, usage, and sentiment of the words used. The exponential use of social networks has served as a great springboard for the dissemination of new uses and meanings of words and expressions used in the texts that opinion makers produce, thus contributing to the construction of a value system which, according to Thompson/Hunston (2000), is built by the community of speakers through evaluation. This system also conveys an ideological component that oozes through the linguistic combinations and constructions of the texts.

When examining the use of crisis vocabulary in influential media such as *The Guardian* or *The New York Times*, we are confronted with a language that refers to events through the use of carefully selected terms that are sourced from the specialized domain of economics, mixed with elements that reference contemporary politics and public life. Like a linguistic transmission belt, the metalanguage is quickly adopted by the public and naturally reused by other media. As a consequence, language adapts to this new reality and evolves to fit the expressive needs of its time. During times of economic crises, financial and economic terms become of widespread use in the media, and attitudes towards them are likely to change. For example, metaphorical expressions such as 'toxic assets' or 'green shoots' have caught on among the general public because they effectively and successfully communicate complex macro-economic concepts, but also convey a certain ideological directionality.

To respond to public demand, the publishing machinery was set in motion to explain the terminology and from 2008 onwards a wide range of lexicographic resources came to light: from glossaries of the crisis to complete terminology dictionaries (e.g., Pinedo/Martínez 2012). These initiatives were intended to shed light on the jargon that flooded front pages and TV news. On the other hand, in many cases journalists explicitly acted as disseminating agents, in an attempt to make the terms less opaque and offer an accessible understanding to their readers. Other economic communication efforts used different strategies, such as reformulating terminology: from paraphrasing to question-answer sets or the use of metaphors. These techniques are an attempt to discuss the context and the world surrounding the terms, thus becoming a means to rework a given discourse (Janot 2012; Rojo López/Orts Llopis 2010).

Regarding this process of linguistic assimilation from the financial power-to-press-to-public chain, Haase (2010) states that, especially in the description of the economic crisis, the data do not speak for themselves, and highlights the enormous importance of the rhetoric used by the mass media when explaining the depth of the economic crisis to their readers. The lexicon used in the spreading of news thus contributes to the overall effect of the crisis presented in the media, as the presentation lacks differentiated background information. This narrative, however, does not work in just one direction. For example, the head of content creation at Oxford Dictionaries conducted a small longitudinal study from field notes on the economic lexicon of the famous Occupy Wall Street protest (Martin 2012). The author finds that while these words achieved wide circulation in the press and spread to other mobilized cities, they did not have a significant impact on the way citizens used English. However, some terms did achieve punctual relevance, for example, 'the 99 %' (in relation to the crisis-affected citizenry), and '1 %' or '1-percent(er)' meaning 'the financial powers'.

The point is that, sometimes, there is an intentional use of specialized language in order to convey not only technical information, but also a certain ideology. In relation to this, Moirand (2007) states that the consumption of media language conveys a collective financial and social cost. On many occasions the media and institutions make an unnecessarily opaque use of terminology, which in turn generates a semantic flurry that includes sentiment. The prevailing ideology of neoliberalism soaks the discourse with its values, and authors such as Massey (2013) are of the opinion that the current neoliberal system has quickly and virtuously taken over the language of everyday life, so that it shapes our conception of ourselves and our way of approaching the world. Thus, in certain environments, train passengers or hospital patients have begun to be naturally referred to as 'customers'. Regarding the speed of these changes, some authors, e.g., Vincent (2011), mentions the existence of rapid changes in the sentiment of words that cannot be reflected in the statism of standard dictionaries. The author labels this phenomenon as *semantic warfare*, where even the mere mention of Wall Street oozes emotion.

In these semantically oriented terms, the polarized use of financial language was questioned by specialists and critics from the onset of the crisis in 2008. In many cases terms with a positive semantic orientation were used to whitewash the beneficial effects that some aspects of the crisis had for big finance, so that they could be better accepted by the public. While the *Troika*, i.e., the European Commission (EC), the European Central Bank (ECB) and the International Monetary Fund (IMF), talked about 'solidarity', this term shifted from referring to cooperation and mutual support to a "solidarity" of firm contracts. The €86 billion solidarity bond to Greece in 2015 meant, first, ironclad conditions for the repayment of that same amount to the borrowers (€50 billion), €25 billion to recapitalize private banks and only €11 billion to revive the country's economy, with the condition of expanding austerity measures, which at the same time made it more dependent on capital injections, thus aggravating the problem of the economy for the country receiving the funds.

Another example is the use of 'structural reforms', the verb 'to reform' has traditionally had a predominantly positive semantic orientation: something that is reformed is assumed to be modified in order to be improved. The collocation with the word 'structural', therefore, should refer to an improvement of a country's structures so that shortcomings are improved. However, the structural reforms (in exchange for its 'solidarity') imposed by the IMF on Greece five years after the first imposition led to a debt growth from 100 to 187 % in relation to its GDP without a qualitative improvement of the economy, rather the opposite: the dismissal of civil servants, the raising of taxes on low incomes, and the privatization of the country's resources for the benefit of foreign investment funds, i.e., the 'markets' (Jiménez Gómez 2015).

Finally, the fascination of capitalist systems with 'growth', without taking into account other factors, measures any economic situation in relation to this concept. This is the case of the popularization of 'negative growth', which has been used to obfuscate the real intended meaning, as a replacement of the term 'recession', which has openly negative connotations. Thus, the negative evaluation is embedded in a structure that is difficult to process both by non-specialized speakers and sentiment analysis algorithms. For example, in Jean-Claude Trichet's (2009) speech, we find the use of this term in sentences in which the negative term is blurred within a non-restrictive clause in the sentence:

> Taking all these measures and their effects into account, as well as the pronouncedly *negative growth* in the first quarter of this year and the most recently published forecasts by public institutions, the risks to this outlook remain broadly balanced.

Alim (2011), in a column for *The New York Times*, reflects on the linguistic influence of the protest movements that arose to defend the population from the onslaught of the crisis. He states that, for example, the Occupy Wall Street phenomenon of 2011 initiated a shift in the narrative of the debate in such a way that it moved some of its terms from the central focus, such as 'debt ceiling' and 'budget balance', and placed others, such as 'inequality' and 'greed', in the limelight as terms of socioeconomic debate. He considers that this change produced variations in the discursive argumentation of the 'establishment' on the reasons for the financial collapse and its consequences. At the same time, the director of the Knight Centre for Digital Media Entrepreneurship at Arizona State University, Gillmor (2011), reflects in *The Guardian* on the evolution of the uses of economic language, and how its connotations in the press often reflect the interests of financial powers. As an example, he mentions that one of the meanings of the verb 'earn' is 'to profit financially', which is always combined in the press with the second meaning assigned to the deserved profit. He then questions whether, given the situation at the time, the enormous profits and assets accumulated during the 1 % crisis merit the use of the word 'earn' in its full meaning, citing the impunity of Wall Street executives during the events that severely affected the world economy. It also questions the partisan use of language that the lobbies propose to the press, a use of specialized language loaded with subjectivity, as in the case of the replacement of the aseptic 'inheritance tax' favored by the use of the subjective 'death tax', with a view to influencing political opinion.

In sum, emotionally biased language, especially when it has been consciously shaped by the media powers, has served as an essential tool for the financial powers and their allies to justify their substantial and controversial gains.

Outside the domain of finance, Massey (2013) notes that, in recent years, the meaning of term 'work' has evolved in such a way that only money transactions are associated with it, thus making invisible traditionally female-oriented unpaid work related to care or creativity, so that these work activities are only appreciated and enjoyed in the intimacy of families and communities. The author reflects that, especially in recent years, 'work' has also become associated with unpleasant connotations, as a necessary evil in order to obtain the reward of attaining consumer goods. She gives other examples of the use of economic terms in the general vocabulary, such as the reference to the terms 'investment' and 'expenditure', and the moral connotations that are implicit in their use. While an 'investment' implies 'activity' and even 'sacrifice', with a view to a better future – positive sentiment – , words with similar meaning, such as 'expenditure', appear to connote an economic burden, that is, negative sentiment. Thus, when we talk about the construction of a school's infrastructure, we will talk about 'investment', but the payment of teachers, the administrative staff, or the canteen staff are described as 'expenditure'.

Finally, it is necessary to highlight the relevance of the press as the main factor in the transmission of opinion. In the press, evidentiality is exposed through the use of specialized language, since that is what assigns greater or lesser relevance to the events narrated (Haase 2010). This use of specialized language has a highly rhetorical, metaphorical and evaluative style. Arrese/Vara-Miguel (2016) review the literature across European languages. Much research during this decade has looked at this issue from multiple perspectives through the use of economic reports for the press in different European languages with similar conclusions: despite the frequent use of idiomatic language, the nature of economic metaphors turns out to be fairly uniform across languages, countries, and newspaper masthead types.

Furthermore, Rojo López/Orts Llópiz (2010) observed in a comparative study between English and Spanish that pre-crisis newspaper articles have a higher number of negative-sentiment metaphors in both languages. In fact, close to fulfilling the role of cliché, the terms are presented as semantic units in media writing as a semiotic concept of the ruptures occurring in the language of the economic domain. In the case of the first study, the economic lexicon of the crisis that was used includes some of the terms to be reviewed in this book, such as 'credit'. These terms were prominently found in the economic sections of newspapers or in economic jargon and, after the crisis, transferred to the general public. Now they seem to be more easily found in everyday language and are often used in evaluative utterances.

As these studies show, newspapers are one of the most interesting textual formats for the analysis of specialized economic and financial language, as they present the discourse among the elites in a way that is accessible to the public while at the same time influencing the rest of the sections. The generic model of mass media has been complemented by analyses of the communication processes among the elites, who make use of specialized publications, and the role of the press as a mediator between the public and the actors who make economic decisions. The information in the articles seems to be within the agenda of the markets and tends to exclude the interests of the public, so that 'financial and business news coverage reproduces the prevalent ideas, norms and values of those who work in these sectors' (Arrese/Vara-Miguel 2016; Davis 2011: 2). The chain of opinions of economic professionals, members of institutions and citizens is largely based on the construction formed from the opinions that others have about these same events based on what is published in the editorial headlines and their different avatars: newspapers, blogs and social networks.

Financial news belong in communication genres considered 'strategic resources' for collective meaning and persuasion (Fairclough 2015). The analysis of voice and opinion in news of an economic or financial nature allows an approximation to the power relations between large publishing and economic groups, since they possess the economic or symbolic influence to be able to expand their points of view with the aim of reaching the general public. Thus, corporations and governments dominate most of the headlines and, as a result, their assessments become the dominant views, especially if they are assimilated by journalists and not questioned by the public. As a consequence, the media become a form of language input to the general public and one of the main transmitters of worldviews (Rocci/Palmieri/Gautier 2015).

3.1 Online content and opinion

The climate of anxiety and discontent that has uniformly permeated the crisis discourse has stoked the need to seek new approaches to be able to study in greater depth the influence of sentiment on communication and markets, looking for new ways to establish ways to measure it reliably and accurately. Sentiment analysis emerged in the first decade of the 21st century to address the problem of opinion mining.

Traditionally, public opinion has been researched through polls and manual textual analysis. Access to this valuable information is costly and only large companies and organizations can afford to carry out these studies. Ordinary citizens and small organizations do not usually have first-hand access to this information. This would be the case of internal opinion polls that, for example, political parties make available to the press if they are favorable to them. For this reason, the rise of the Web 2.0 revolutionized the world of information and communications by democratizing them and making them more horizontal. On the other hand, the Web provides greater propagation and access of information to media of all kinds and origins. This includes everything, from the new digital platforms of media empires to new grassroots methods, such as community radio and television stations and "traditional", web 1.0 online media, as well as a plethora of podcasts and blogs. Thus, in addition to professional media, we cannot ignore in this section what has been called *user-generated content*, or UGC, which, in relation to online opinion, becomes 'electronic word-of-mouth' (eWOM), a 2.0 replacement of the traditional concept, as it provides verifiable information about any entity from peers instead of advertising offered by the service or product provider itself (Cheung/Thadani 2012).

UGC is understood as digital materials created by users in a non-amateur way to disseminate ideas or content for the sake of sharing, or to influence others. This content can be of different nature: blog posts, comments section on news sites, restaurant review pages, podcasts, etc. Not surprisingly, given the portentous plasticity of capitalism, in the last decade thousands of 'influencers' have emerged, users who semi-professionally promote 'sponsored' products based on reviews and opinions, or even companies that generate content that simulates amateur aesthetics for purely commercial purposes. Both UGC and editorial materials of this Web generation are a good source of information that can be extracted by computational techniques, becoming a source of real language samples rich in opinions (Balasubramaniam 2009).

Within Natural Language Processing (NLP), a specific field of study has evolved that focuses on processing opinionated text to extract the sentiment that is expressed in it. Sentiment analysis systems offer a number of advantages over traditional methods, such as the analysis of financial or public opinion reports, or periodically published indices such as the Eurozone Economic Sentiment Indicator, among others. Currently, we can have up-to-the-minute sentiment information directly available on the different economic sectors from the opinions expressed in the texts of the desired sources: press, institutions or companies (Malo et al. 2014).

In Chapters 5 and 6 we describe the methods and tools of sentiment analysis in detail, but before we do that, we need to clarify what exactly is understood by *evaluative language*.

4 Evaluative language

Both emotions and opinions condition the way humans communicate with each other and, to a large extent, determine their actions. Evaluative language, according to Stubbs (1986) is used to express personal beliefs and take viewpoints, to express agreement or disagreement with other people, to establish alliances, contracts and commitments and, ultimately, to reflect a value system, dissociate the speaker from certain points of view and consciously stay vague or noncommittal to what is being expressed (Du Bois 2007; Hunston 2011; Moreno-Ortiz/Pérez-Hernández 2014).

In everyday language use, there are certain words whose potential to express opinion is not limited by the context. For example, adjectives like 'excellent' or expressions like 'it's a shame that...' invariably express opinion in any context or conceptual domain. However, other expressions have a more referential content, but their meaning includes an element of opinion that can be activated (or not) according to the context and communicative situation in which they appear. For example, the word 'jam' can be understood as 'a lot of traffic' + 'bad'. Opinion is an essential language feature in order to fully describe the meaning of a text (Thompson/Hunston 2000).

The study of evaluative language has attracted the interest of scholars in multiple disciplines: from various fields in the humanities, and social sciences, such as philosophy, sociology, and political science, to engineering, specifically data science, affective computing, and artificial intelligence. The latter has accompanied the emergence of the Web 2.0, especially through social networks that allow their users to disseminate opinions, emotions, and evaluations, on a scale that is both horizontal and global (Benamara/Taboada/Mathieu 2017).

The humanistic study of values goes back to classical dissertations on ethics and rhetoric, for example, in the study of the universality of the *Form of the Good* in its Platonic sense. With the emergence of German idealism, Kant (1785) considers moral value as an absolute, unique and universally identifiable value. This universality of values was challenged by American pragmatism, e.g., Dewey's Theory of Valuation (1939), which denied the existence of intrinsic value as an inherent property of things, relativizing its valuation and, therefore, requiring an in-depth study of the discourse and intersubjective nature of values.

The study of human value systems is a very complex field that can be tackled to a large extent from the study of evaluative language in use. From a linguistic perspective, different analytical frameworks have been proposed that attempt to establish a model of the relationship between factual or referential content and affective or expressive content.

However, the task of identifying evaluative language is not a simple one; since the 20th century some linguistic models have been proposed, including *representative/expressive* (Buhler 1934), *descriptive/expressive* (Lyons 1977), *ideational/interpersonal* (Halliday et al. 2014), *expressive/relational* (Fairclough 2015). Although most authors have focussed on different text types and features of evaluative language, some theories have offered more concise accounts of the nature of attitudinal language, such as *modality and modulation* (Halliday et al. 2014); *evaluative orientations* (Lemke 1998); *stance* (Conrad/Biber 2000), *evaluation* (Alba-Juez/Thompson 2014; Bednarek 2006, 2008a) or *appraisal* (J. R. Martin/White 2005).

This chapter summarizes some of the most salient concepts and associated terms that have been used by different authors in the study of evaluative language. Although these terms and concepts share a vast working space (and in many cases can be considered roughly equivalent), it is possible to discuss at length the differences between these terms according to the authors that have used them. What lies beneath are the different conceptions of what *evaluation* is and the salient features that the authors are interested in. In the following section we offer a detailed review of terms, concepts and approaches related to evaluation in language.

4.1 Terms and concepts in evaluative language

Although similar in nature, the terminological systems used to describe evaluative language have been diverse. This section will briefly describe and discuss the main terms used throughout the literature of the last three decades and address the question of the definition of the term 'appraisal' throughout the literature.

One of the most long-standing studies is that by Chafe (1986) which takes as its starting point the scarcity of work on evaluation in Anglistics compared to the existing literature in Eastern languages. According to this author, this is because it was initially assumed that evidentiality was relegated to implicit (para)linguistic elements such as tone, duration, or stress, and so the groundwork was laid for the discussion of the first terms used to reflect concepts related to the expression of evaluation. He defined 'evidentiality' as the attitudes expressed by the speaker towards knowledge: its reliability, the way it is known, and how adequate the speaker considers its utterances. Thus, the enunciation and the physical reality of its context are aligned. The author distinguishes three aspects of evidentiality:

1. Reliability of knowledge, intrinsic and eminently adverbial: he uses particles such as 'maybe', 'probably', 'surely'.
2. Mode of knowledge (belief, induction and hearsay): the first with constructions such as '*I* think' or '*I* guess', the second with 'must' or 'seem' and the third with modals such as 'should', 'could', or 'presumably'.
3. Source of knowledge (belief, evidence, verbal report and hypothesis): expressed mainly from verbs related to the senses such as 'see', 'hear', or 'feel'.

According to this, some authors (Saurí/Pustejovsky 2009; Szarvas et al. 2008) consider that despite being an important factor in, for example, detecting the source of opinion and its reliability, evidentiality has not received much attention in sentiment analysis, despite providing a set of useful resources to determine the reliability of an opinion. Some aspects of this, however, are captured in the engagement system within appraisal theory, which will be reviewed later.

Labov (1984) used the term *intensity* as the emotional expression of the social orientation towards the linguistic proposition; in other words, the subject's commitment to that proposition. A distinction is thus made between verbal elements that reflect the strength and reliability of a proposition in positive terms ('absolutely', 'completely', 'extremely'); and the mere marking of certainty in a proposition ('for sure', 'really').

Stance is a broad term used in two different ways in the literature. Biber and colleagues published a series of papers (Biber/Finegan 1988, 1989; Conrad/Biber 2000), which tackled evaluative language from a then novel computational approach: Corpus Linguistics. They describe *stance* as the expression of the speaker's attitudes, feelings and judgment, while reflecting evidentiality devices used to express commitment to the message, as well as *affect*, which in addition to personal attitudes, such as emotions, sentiments or mood, reflects the speaker's positive or negative evaluation (Ochs/Schieffelin 1989).

By studying the London-Lund Corpus, Biber/Finegan (1989) created a classification of *stance* into six categories, accompanied by their most frequent lexicogrammatical features and genres: *emphatic expression of affect, faceless stance, interactional evidentiality, expository expression of doubt, predictive persuasion, controversial oral persuasion*. From here, they distinguished two pragmatic functions of stance: *affect* and *evidentiality*, and distinguished two semantic axes: *positive/negative* (for *affect*) and *certainty/doubt* (for *evidentiality*).

A decade later, Conrad/Biber (2000) simplified the classification and distinguished three types of stance: *epistemic stance, attitudinal stance* and *stylistic stance*. The first indicates the degree of certainty of the speaker and is manifested in five ways: (a) degree of certainty or doubt about the proposition ('perhaps', 'certainly', etc.), (b) commenting on the reality of the proposition ('actually', 'in fact', etc.), (c) indicating vagueness or imprecision ('sort of', 'nearly', etc.), (d) identifying the original source of information ('according to') and (e) identifying the perspective of the speaker ('apparently', 'from our perspective'). *Attitudinal stance* expresses judgments and opinions about what is being expressed ('fortunately', 'most surprising of all', etc.). Finally, *stylistic stance* refers to the speaker's comments on the presentation of the clause ('honestly', 'simply put', etc.).

A paradigm shift was the study of *stance-taking*, which in addition to taking into account the speaker's utterance, reviews the human communicative activity behind it. Du Bois (2007) explains the concept by means of a triangle metaphor. The *stance triangle* was designed to represent how communication takes place during dialogue in an act that is composed of *evaluation, positioning, and alignment*. In this triangle (see Figure 4.1) Subject 1 evaluates an Object and thus takes a particular kind of stance; then Subject 2 aligns to that stance by also evaluating the Object, positioning themselves towards the Object in relation to Subject 1's positioning. In this triangle, it is necessary to take into account the relationship of the subjective / ideological stance ('where you and I position ourselves') with the intersubjective / interactional stance ('how you and I relate to each other').

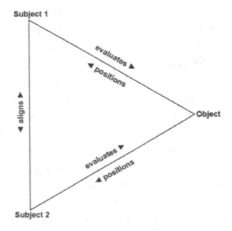

Figure 4.1. Du Bois's stance triangle

The study of *modality*, which does not refer exclusively to the use of modal verbs, has also been a recurrent theme to study the opinion regarding the probability of occurrence of certain characteristics mentioned in the discourse. Halliday et al. (2014) and Perkins (1982) offer an comprehensive review of the lexicogrammatical framework of the modality system. In systemic-functional approaches, Halliday et al. (2014) reflect on the need to separate modality from attitudinal meaning and explore it further by establishing two subcategories: *modalization* (related to *probability* and *usuality*) and *modulation* (related to obligation and inclination). The authors place both meanings within the *interpersonal metafunctional* category. This category also includes other concepts, such as the speaker's mood, and does not contain a specific subdivision that encompasses these two concepts exclusively.

Attitude is a cover term that refers to a distributed network of mental and emotional states, affect, beliefs, certainty, commitment, dispositions, emotions, ideology, stance, state of mind, or any other related inner condition, whether transient or permanent (Jullian 2009). As a concept, *attitude* is key in the study of evaluation, as it is at the centre of a major theoretical framework regarding evaluation: Martin/White's (2005) Appraisal Theory, as an expansion of the attitudinal meaning of the interpersonal metafunction of Halliday's Systemic Functional Linguistics (SFL). The key assumption of this theory is that in every sentence, speakers express their approval or disapproval, either directly or indirectly. This evaluative component, *attitude*, is divided into three categories: *affect, judgement,* and *appreciation*. Not only does Appraisal Theory provide a very rich description of the different aspects of evaluation and subjective positioning, but it is perhaps one of the most widely accepted, with a large body of literature using it as an analysis framework and a reference for linguistically-motivated sentiment analysis implementations (Benamara/Taboada/Mathieu 2017).

The study of evaluative language and the associated concepts and terms that we have reviewed in this section (*evidentiality, modality, stance,* and *attitude*) is related to the language of emotions. Bednarek (2008a) differentiates between *emotion talk* and *emotional talk*. The former consists of expressions denoting affect/emotion, e.g., 'love', 'hate', 'joy', 'envy', 'sadness', 'disgust', etc., more complex expressions such as 'a broken heart'. Emotional speech refers to linguistic and extralinguistic elements that serve to express affect or emotion (e.g., exclamations, intensifications). In relation to Martin/White's (2005) framework, while *affect* (in particular, its mental processes and states) fits better in emotion speech, *appraisal* and *judgment* can potentially be treated within the *emotional talk* paradigm. On this, Bednarek is of the opinion that it is necessary to establish clear boundaries between affect and emotion, as she considers that evaluation does not necessarily reflect the actual emotions or feelings of the speakers.

4.2 Definition of evaluation

Following Thompson/Hunston (2000: 5), we take the term 'evaluation' as:

> the broad cover term for the expression of the speaker or writer's attitude or stance towards, viewpoint on, or feelings about the entities or propositions that he or she is talking about. That attitude may relate to certainty or obligation or desirability or any of a number of other sets of values.

Alba-Juez/Thompson (2014: 13) updated this definition and expanded it taking into account the theoretical innovations developed throughout this decade. The revised definition is framed beyond the text and evidences its participation in complex dialogic processes:

> a dynamical subsystem of language, permeating all linguistic levels and involving the expression of the speaker's or writer's attitude or stance towards, viewpoint on, or sentiments about the entities or propositions that s/he is talking about, which entails relational work including the (possible and prototypically expected and subsequent) response of the hearer or (potential) audience. This relational work is generally related to the speaker's and/or the hearer's personal, group or cultural set of values.

Given the diversity of theories and approaches to evaluative language, Hunston (2011) lists six points of consensus among the different approaches to evaluative language. They are as follows:

1. Evaluation is subjective and intersubjective. Regarding the former: evaluative sentences share personal opinions and evaluative utterances are endorsed only by their sender. On intersubjectivity, we can relate it to Du Bois's (2007) triangle, or to Martin/White's (2005) speaker-listener alignment. On this,

Hunston (2011) considers that evaluation serves to build and maintain human relationships.
2. Evaluation implies a shared ideology between speaker and listener. Although evaluation is personal and subjective, it takes place within a minimal ideological and value framework shared by both actors and effective even if the speakers disagree when expressing their opinions.
3. Evaluative meaning is realized by a wide range of lexical items and other elements. Although different schools differ on what the term *evaluation* encompasses (e.g., whether or not modality should be included), agreement exists that the focus is on what is desirable and undesirable. Another point of agreement is that evaluation depends to a large extent on context, and that the different elements that constitute evaluative language are so broad that listing them is hardly feasible if at all. Some lexical items that when contextualized can indicate evaluation: nouns (e.g., 'success'), verbs (e.g., 'fail'), adjectives (e.g., 'excellent'), adverbs (e.g., 'sadly') or multiword expressions such as 'number one'.
4. Evaluation is contextual and cumulative. If a word is potentially positive in isolation, its polarity cannot be determined with certainty without other semantic and pragmatic aspects (e.g., negation, irony). On the other hand, evaluative meanings tend to coalesce, so we can recognize a segment as evaluative by detecting that different evaluative elements act together.
5. Every evaluation implies a target, an object and a source. These concepts are central to the aforementioned Du Bois's (2007) stance triangle and are included in Liu's (2015) five-factor opinion system, as these factors are key elements for sentiment analysis.
6. The task of identifying evaluation is complicated by subjectivity, i.e., the 'ideological glasses' that we see through whenever we read a text, and often determine whether we consider a text to be evaluative or factual in nature.

Goźdź-Roszkowski/Hunston (2016) add the following considerations:

Functions of evaluation 43

1. Evaluation represents language that can be subjective or attitudinal and that can be distinguished from objective or factual.
2. Evaluation is multifunctional, executing roles to interpret relationships between participants in an interaction and to structure discourse. For example, it can serve the purpose of changing the subject.
3. Evaluation can be *inscribed/explicit* or *evoked/implied*. In order to detect which axis it fits into, local grammars and registers may be necessary.
4. Although the basis of evaluation is the polarity good/bad, there are patterns of a different nature.
5. The study of evaluation should tackle the concepts of *heteroglossia* and *intertextuality*, as it can be carried out by means of expressions attributed to other speakers.
6. Evaluative language is a key field for referencing and interpreting different ideologies (*hegemonic* and *resistant*) since the *inscribed* or *implicit* evaluation presupposes a shared set of values.

4.3 Functions of evaluation

Given the existence of so many frameworks, visions and approaches to evaluative language, it is worth asking the question 'why is evaluation so important as a subject of study?'. Hunston (2011) points out that any evaluative act uttered by a speaker has at least one of three functions: (a) the expression of the speaker's opinion in a way that it reflects their value system and that of their community, (b) the construction and maintenance of speaker-listener relations, and (c) the organization of discourse.

Obviously, the expression of opinion is the most frequent function, since this is how alignment – sentiment about a specific topic – can be expressed. The identification of what the speaker thinks transcends the ideas of the individual: each act of evaluation has a common value system as its backdrop, and each act of evaluation contributes to its collective construction. This value system is one more cog in the ideological machine behind each text. Therefore, text analysis allows us to learn more about a community's ideology. Although these are not explicit in the observation of evaluative texts, they allow us to know (according to the voice of the text) what codes or statements are expected and desirable, what is good, what is bad, what should and should not happen.

The second function of evaluation is the construction and maintenance of relationships between speaker and listener. This social construct has been studied in relation to three axes of observation: *manipulation*, *hedging*, and *politeness*. In each of these areas, the speaker exploits evaluative resources to construct a particular type of relationship with the reader. Evaluation is often used with the aim of persuading the listener so that the latter is persuaded in a particular direction. For example, if the speaker considers a certain issue to be 'a problem', they must necessarily use language to label the statement as conflicting. It is difficult for the reader not to accept this perception of the problem as such, if only one point of view is expressed dialogically. From here, the listener should increase their attention levels to extract the underlying viewpoint or ideology about the problem. Since much information relevant to evaluation is taken for granted and omitted, the speaker must show whether their evaluation is the main point of a discourse through different textual organization strategies. Usually, the listener does not take a stand and decides if they agree with what is being evaluated, and assumes the position without being critical. (Hoey 2000).

Francis (1986) indicates that certain discourse labels play a very important role when carrying out the task of summarizing, distributing the text and maintaining levels of alignment between what the listener and the speaker consider acceptable. These discourse labels can, in a simple way, summarize ('these words', 'this question', 'to sum up') or evaluate ('this claim', 'this nonsense'). There are discourse organization functions that play a key factor in influencing the listener, e.g., when information considered hegemonic is offered in a factual way, the listener lets down their guard and does not question its validity. Thus, the less evaluation is concealed in a given clause, the more successful will the text be when manipulating the reader. One of the most frequent interpersonal phenomena here is *hedging*, whereby the degree of certainty of a statement is related to a degree of prior shared knowledge.

For example, in academic writing, we can speak both of discursive elements (words like 'insignificant', 'somewhat'), or expressions like 'I'm not an expert but...'. The use of these elements guarantees a final version of the statement negotiated in a more precise way through modifications, which facilitates the alignment between interlocutors. On the other hand, there are some textual factors that make alignment more difficult. An example of this would be the addition of adversative clauses to the discourse in anticipation of conflicting points that may add difficulty to the comprehension of an enunciation (Hunston 2011).

Finally, in addition to aligning interlocutors, evaluative segments are also used to organize discourse so that one can say 'this part is the beginning of the text', 'this part indicates how the argument fits', and 'this section is the end of our interaction'. Hunston (2011) mentions that Sinclair already discussed evaluation and its organizing role in discourse. From a teacher's 'Yes, that's right' after a contribution in class, for example, to the way a speaker highlights the key points of their speech as 'the interesting part of this is...'. In addition to organizing the narrative of a text, he cites authors such as Labov (1972), who considers evaluation to be the main part of a text (literally, 'the point' of it), since he believes that a story cannot exist without some kind of evaluation. The narrator must emphasize why these facts should be told and why they should be paid attention to. Although evaluation occurs throughout the narrative in a more or less open way, it takes on relevance and is preeminent in different parts of the narrative: at the beginning, in the complication, and in the resolution. In conclusion, he indicates that the evaluation allows the narrative to be realized, since it turns it into an interactive text and makes it fulfil its communicative function.

4.4 Markers of evaluation

Evaluation is considered conceptually comparative, subjective and sentiment-laden. It follows that identifying it involves detecting markers of comparison, subjectivity and social values. From the studies described so far in this chapter it should be clear that evaluative language presents difficulties in its analysis because there is no clear set of linguistic forms (whether grammatical, lexical or discursive) that cover the full range of evaluative utterances. Still, some recurrent patterns have been identified in the literature. For example, a large proportion of adjectives and adverbs express evaluative meaning; also, their patterns are almost always associated with evaluative expressions. Similarly, evaluation is often expressed in terms of comparisons, which does not necessarily involve a comparative grammatical pattern (Hunston 2011).

Although there is a high degree of agreement in determining the evaluative meaning of words based on introspection and shared experience within a community of speakers, establishing criteria to distinguish evaluative elements from the rest is a highly complex task. The author illustrates this with the examples 'Jane is a genius' and 'Jane is a student'. The first statement can be said to be of an evaluative nature, since 'genius' is a noun that positively qualifies the subject by locating them above the average in terms of intelligence, a socially valued feature. In the second example, que quality of being a 'student' can be said to be an objective fact that refers to a person's occupation, while in some specific contexts it can have a positive connotation (someone who is part of an intellectual elite) or a negative one (disorderly, irresponsible, immature). Corpus linguistics allows us to study the contexts in which such words occur and thus ascertain the actual evaluative quality of a word.

Beyond the use of the evaluative lexicon, grammatical patterns also play an important role in the expression of evaluation. Labov (1972, 1984) was one of the pioneers in the detection of grammatical patterns. He pointed out the existence of four types of linguistic elements with evaluative meaning:

- *Intensifiers*: such as gestures or expressive prosody, quantifiers, repetitions, ritual expressions.
- *Comparators*: such as negatives, futures, modals, quasi-modals, questions, imperatives, disjunctive clauses, superlatives, and comparatives.
- *Correlatives*: including progressives, adjunctive particles, and attributives.
- *Explicatives*: such as the subordinating particles 'while', 'though', 'since', or 'because'.

Stubbs (1986) discusses evaluative grammar from modal grammar viewpoint. He takes as a starting point a concise exploration of the interaction between lexis, grammar, and pragmatic knowledge that allows us to highlight some of the evaluative elements present in an utterance:

- Expressions of the origin of propositions.
- Phrases that limit commitment, such as 'if I can'.
- Ways of being explicit through performative utterances or the conscious use of vagueness during the speech act.
- The choice of the stative or progressive aspect of cognitive verbs.
- The modal meaning of private verbs, which express states (e.g., 'believe') or intellectual actions (e.g., 'discover') that are not observable.
- Logical connectors: (e.g., 'and', 'but', 'or', 'if', 'because').
- Past tense indicating temporal remoteness (e.g., 'I did wonder if I might ask you a question').
- References to the future.
- Tag questions.

Biber/Finegan (1989) made a list of so-called *stance markers*, a series of lexical items selected from word types and other categories that are divided into *affect* (positive or negative) and *evidentiality* (certainty and doubt).

Table 4.1 Affect and evidentiality categories. Adapted from Biber/Finegan (1989)

Affect	
Positive	*Negative*
Adjectives: 'fortunate', 'amazing'	'shocked', 'unnatural'
Verbs: 'enjoy', 'please'	'dread', 'embarrass'
Adverbs: 'happily', 'conveniently', 'luckily'...	'disturbingly', 'sadly'

Evidentiality	
Certainty	*Doubt*
Adjectives: 'impossible', 'obvious', 'true'...	'alleged', 'dubious', 'uncertain'
Verbs: 'conclude', 'demonstrate'	'assume', 'indicate'
Adverbs: 'assuredly', 'indeed', 'without doubt...'	'allegedly', 'perhaps', 'supposedly'
Emphatic: 'of course', 'really', 'so + ADJ'	Hedges: 'at about', 'maybe', 'sort of'
Predictive modals: 'will', 'shall'	Possibility modals: 'might', 'could'
	Necessity modals: 'ought', 'should'

4.5 Evaluation in journalistic genres

The news genre has well-defined priorities when it comes to expressing the desirability of an evaluation. After all, good/bad evaluations are broad elements that depend on the value system and preferences behind the text. For example, in some situations living and experiencing may trump lack of comfort (for an alpinist, for example, the reward of the unique scenery of the Orobic Alps is worth the effort and safety risk). Thus, the genre of a text determines the priorities underlying the type evaluation: certainty vs. good/bad evaluations or importance vs expectations.

Bednarek (2006), later revised in Bednarek/Caple (2012), proposed a specific framework for this genre aimed at detecting evaluative segments within the text through a set of parameters. These parameters create a conceptual framework to concisely study the markers of a highly evaluative discourse type such as journalistic texts. This framework is organized across ten axes:

1. *Un/importance* answers the question 'how important is this?'. For example: 'This is a major event.'
2. *In/comprehensibility,* where the news actors evaluate whether the quality of the information is good, or whether there is vagueness. For example: 'It's impossible to pin down the reasons for this success.'
3. *Im/possibility, in/ability* is related to the deontic modality and concerned with what is (or is not) possible when assessing a situation or an event. For example: 'They've not been able to make a go of it financially.'
4. *Un/necessity* is related to the deontic and dynamic modality, i.e., constructions, modal verbs, verbs, adverbs and adjectives expressing what is (or is not) necessary in a way that it explains the consideration of what should or should not be done. For example: 'The dispute between Belarus and Russia should act as a wakeup call to the EU commission.'
5. *Emotivity*, which refers to the evaluation by the source of opinion of a situation as positive or negative on the basis of aesthetic or moral values of desirability and has a broad

ideological background. This characteristic is the one that more directly relates to our work, and goes hand in hand with the Attitude parameter of the Appraisal Theory. This axis is key in journalistic news because editorial titles construct stories in line with their target audience in a way that suggests to their readers what is desirable according to a series of values.

6. *(Un)genuiness* or *(in)/authenticity*: here the reporter values the authenticity of the news elements. For example: 'But there was a question of how much was genuine weakness and how much was due to these factors'.
7. *Reliability*, which is directly related to the epistemic modality (modals such as 'will' or 'could'), and refers to certain elements that evaluate the probability of something happening. For example: 'The bank is not likely to be the only one affected by the credit crunch.'
8. *Un/expectedness*, which expresses how expected a certain event is, including conjunctions ('but', 'yet'), adverbs ('although', 'even', etc.), etc.. In general terms, it is similar to the negation set of contextual valence shifters of Polanyi/Zaenen (2006).
9. *Evidentiality* refers to the expressions that indicate the bases on which the enunciations and information are founded. For example, the use of direct speech to validate the news source.
10. *Mental state* refers to emotions, beliefs, expectations, etc., in order to increase the newsworthiness of sharing these feelings. For example, 'growing frustration', 'refusing', 'cast doubts', etc.

This framework does not distinguish between lexical and grammatical factors, nor does it go into an in-depth discussion of the boundaries between evaluation and opinion that, in contrast, other authors (notably Liu 2015) have discussed with a view to conducting sentiment analysis. However, it provides clear evidence of the difficulty to distinguish evaluative utterances from factual ones, and points out the fact that there are statements that are apparently not evaluative and yet clearly contain a certain semantic orientation. For example the sentence 'oil prices were raised' is formally factual, but may nevertheless convey a certain sentiment that will depend on the reader (e.g., an oil company shareholder or a motorist).

Taking into account all the evaluation frameworks we have reviewed so far, we can conclude that, in addition to the classic lexicogrammatical evaluative markers related to the expression of modality and affect, it is necessary to take into account evaluation as a fundamental element in the organization of a text. Moreover, it is necessary to relate these elements to markers that compare reality with subjective elements of desirability that are relative to the individual or to the construction of a global evaluative framework of a community of speakers.

This chapter has comprehensively summarized the state of the art in the study of evaluative language from an eminently linguistic point of view. The study of *evaluation*, *affect* or *appraisal*, among other terms, is a multidisciplinary issue that involves, in addition to the study of language, knowledge of psychology or sociology.

However, such refined approaches, of which Appraisal Theory is probably the best exemplar, are destined to be put into practice in a predominantly qualitative manner through manual analysis work performed by experts in a very thorough manner. Due to their nature, it is complicated to implement automated solutions that permit practical natural language processing (2015). This is why simpler but formalizable models have been proposed that attempt to serve as a basis for the automatic treatment of evaluation and opinion. We explore these in the following chapter.

5 Formal models for the study of evaluative language

5.1 Liu's model

To systematically and formally address the problem of opinion analysis, Liu (2015) defines a quintuple that enumerates the factors that constitute an opinion: *entity, aspect, sentiment, opinion holder*, and *time* (e, a, s, h, t). According to this framework, an opinion typically consists of two clearly distinguishable elements: a target entity e and a sentiment s, which can be positive or negative, about which an opinion is expressed. When an opinion is only about the entity, the special aspect GENERAL is used to denote it (e and a represent the opinion target in this case); in all other cases a certain aspect of the entity is being evaluated. To resolve the complexities presented by the assignment of sentiment to an entity, the various phrases or words expressing sentiment have syntactic relations observable by means of local grammars. The first difficulty is one of classification and data structuring, since it is necessary to determine whether there are one or multiple entities and aspects. Different strategies can be designed to establish the correct connections between sentiments and the entities and aspects they refer to so that algorithms can be systematized. It is important to understand that in this model there is only one only obligatory element in the quintuple (s); for example aspect may or may not be the target of the analysis, when it is we call it *aspect-based sentiment analysis* or *feature-based sentient analysis*, when it isn't it is sometimes called *entity-based sentiment analysis* (Liu 2015).

Therefore, in this model, *sentiment* is distinguished from *opinion*. An opinion includes sentiment as the one indispensable component, but others play a role too, especially the target of the opinion (entity or aspect). Further, the sentiment of an opinion is represented by the tuple (y, o, i), where y is the sentiment type, o is the sentiment orientation and i is the sentiment intensity. Various types of sentiment can be distinguished. There are classifications based on linguistics, psychology, and consumer research. Liu (2015) chooses a classification based on consumer research, as it is simple and straightforward to apply in practice. Consumer research broadly divides sentiment into two classes: *rational sentiment* and *emotional sentiment* (Chaudhuri 2006). The former refers to reasoning and utilitarian attitudes, whereas the latter are motivated by emotional responses and people's psychological states of mind.

As for the resulting sentiment information, there are two main approaches depending on the level of granularity of the sentiment intensity. The assigned sentiment values can be polarized in nature, often referred to in the literature as the *Thumbs up / Thumbs down* approach: positive, negative, and sometimes neutral (Pang/Lee/ Vaithyanathan 2002) or graded (the *Seeing Stars* approach), such that it presents a score based on a scale, e.g., on a [1, 5] scale, 1 would be negative, 2 slightly negative, 3 neutral, 4 slightly positive, and 5 very positive (Pang/Lee 2005).

The polarity (or orientation) and intensity of a lexical item can be modulated by interacting with other contextual items in a way that is determined from a compositional process that captures the way opinion expressions interact with each other through the application of different intensification, attenuation or inversion operators. Negative adverbials are the example of inversion, for example in the sentence 'He's not a sympathetic person', in which positive polarity is inverted by the adverb 'not'. Another interesting factor is that certain words considered neutral, in combination with other words, can change their polarity. For example, the lexical units 'steady' and 'job' have a neutral sentiment, but together, they are often considered positive (Haas/Versley 2015). The latter point will be addressed in more depth in the Chapter.

While sentiment is straightforward when explicit, it may be not so easy to detect when it is implicit. It is possible to find ironic evaluations that bring the opposite sentiment to that expressed literally to so-called *thwarted expectations*, in which several negative opinions chained together conclude with a positive evaluation, in a way that provokes a surprising reaction in the listener, as in the case exposed by Benamara et al. (2017):

(1) The characters are unpleasant. The scenario is totally absurd. The decoration seems to be made of cardboard. But, all these elements make the charm of this TV series.

The opinion holder (h) refers to the subject that expresses their opinion about an entity. For many systems, this value is important when trying to select the information, because depending on who the person or organization that provides this opinion is, may determine its influence and/or credibility. In texts such as product reviews, the source of the opinion is usually the author of the publication; in others, such as news or narratives, determining the source of the opinion may prove to be a highly complex task which, and, in many cases, may be irrelevant.

Finally, the time of the opinion (t) is a reference to the date and time of publication of the opinion. In applications that target the analysis of time series or language change, as is the case in this book, time may be essential in the analysis of sentiment, as we want to observe the trends and the evolution of the sentiment towards an entity over a given interval. Thus, different methodologies can be performed e.g., observing seasonality and establishing causal relationships between sentiment and external phenomena (Farzindar/Inkpen 2015; Fernández-Cruz/Baixauli-Pérez 2018).

It is also relevant to describe how the entity element of the quintuple is defined. In Liu's model, an *entity* (e) is a product, service, topic, person organization, issue, or event that is described with a pair (T, W), where T is the hierarchy (or ontology) of parts and subparts that the entity is made up of, and W is the set of *attributes* that the entity has. In addition, each part or subpart can have its own hierarchical set of attributes. Liu (2015) proposes this example to illustrate this: an SLR camera has a set of parts (lens, battery, viewfinder, etc.) and these in turn have a subset of attributes or aspects e.g., in battery life, charging time, image quality, etc. The parts fall within a hierarchical description of entities based on a part-whole relationship. In the camera example, the root node is the camera model and the rest of the nodes would correspond to its parts and subparts. Then he goes on to define a number of further elements that may be relevant in finer-grained analysis of opinions. Other elements that deepen the completeness of the study and classification of the opinion are the following:

- Reason for opinion: the cause or explanation for the outcome of the opinion. A product or service provider may be interested in the causes that determine a given sentiment.
- Qualifier of opinion: limits or modifies the meaning of the opinion. Let's take the headline as an example: 'There is no penalty too harsh for a banker', where a negative sentiment is used for a conviction, but it does not refer to all penalties because the negative sentiment is limited to bankers.

If we take into account all of the above, up to eight factors are come into play, which involves a high level of complexity, so for practical tasks, only a subset of these elements are targeted. A high level of hierarchization is often impractical and inefficient in general. An extreme example of the above would be the model by Salas-Zárate et al.(2016), which proposes an ontology system using the standard Web Ontology Language to analyze entities in the financial domain with, among others, 247 classes and 38 object properties. Achieving a thorough level of detail is a highly complex task and, contrary to what might be expected, given the creativity of natural language, it does not produce great benefits.

Liu (2015) proposes to simplify ontologies in sentiment analysis so that the logical structure of parts and attributes goes only two levels deep, where the lower one is the aspect level. In a simplified tree, the root node would refer to the entity, and the second level would include the various aspects of the entity. On the other hand, very high levels of simplification in the analysis can result in a significant loss of information. This is the case, for example, in the analysis of the sentence proposed by the author:

(2) The INK of this printer is EXPENSIVE.

According to the author, the adjective 'expensive' in this sentence is an evaluation with negative sentiment in relation to the attribute 'price' of the ink aspect. First, the expressive ink-printer relationship should be understood as a nested part-whole relationship. This sentence does not mention the price of the printer as an overall entity, but one of its parts, so negative sentiment should not be attributed to the 'price' aspect of the printer. Otherwise, if only the ink aspect is relevant in a given study, then it should be treated as an entity outside the printer hierarchy.

As a conclusion, Benamara et al. (2017) consider that this model covers the main elements to cope in a practical way with implementations dedicated to the treatment of evaluative language. From a linguistic point of view, especially when compared to Appraisal Theory (Martin/White 2005), this purely formal model may turn out to be static given the difficulty of dealing with evaluative language in scenarios where many of the elements are embedded in the context and therefore not verbalized.

5.2 Benamara's model

Benamara et al. (2017) propose a new evaluative model based on the dynamic semantics paradigm of Kamp/Reyle (1993), Liu (2012, 2015) and Polanyi/Zaenen's (2006) Contextual Valence Shifters system, with a view to detecting and formalizing the pragmatic and discursive aspects of evaluation. This evaluation model builds on previous linguistic models in order to find a simple theoretical implementation that serves as an adaptor to the discipline of sentiment analysis.

The model is represented as a dynamic, rather than static, model, in which the presence of elements depends on linguistic and extra-linguistic factors. The system considers the components Ω and I, the former being similar to Liu's (2015) definition of opinion, to which he adds a set of contextual rules. The first of the elements is $\Omega = (e, a, s, h)$, which is a tuple representing the evaluative language properties (*entity, aspect, sentiment* and *opinion holder*); if time is relevant, a fifth item (t) can be added to the tuple. Sentiment (s) is further composed of a tuple (*span, category, pol, val*), i.e., evaluative span, semantic category, polarity and valence. Here sentiment s is structured in similar terms to Liu's, however, this only applies to text spans composed of explicitly subjective parts, such as adjectives, verbs, nouns, adverbs and emojis, and excludes local operators at the sentence level. The authors ground this with the aim of separating the decontextualized value of *s* from its contextualized interpretation, considered part of the extrinsic properties of evaluation (as will be seen below in I). In addition, polarity (*pol*) includes any type of classification: e.g., positive-negative, pro/con, positive/neutral/negative, or any number of stars on a scale.

The second component of this model corresponds to the set of functions $I = \{F_1, \ldots, F_n\}$ that gathers the extrinsic properties of the evaluation, adjusting or adapting the previous values of Ω as soon as it occurs in a given context such that

$$\forall F_i \in I, F_i: \Omega \rightarrow Update(\Omega)$$

This set of functions is abstract and can be adapted according to the need of the evaluation system by adding or omitting the necessary functions to be included in I, so that users can specify them according to the needs and available natural language processing techniques.

This set of functions will act as complex update operators at discourse organization levels (sentence, document, and beyond the document). The interpretation of these functions will reflect the influence they have on evaluative utterances. Thus, at the sentence level, a function can be designed to reflect negation or modality. At the document level, the functions will take into account the argumentative relations to update the polarity that a given evaluation previously had. For illustration purposes, the authors propose the following example:

(3) What a great animated movie. I was so scared the whole time that I didn't even move out of my seat.

In the first sentence 'great' updates the sentiment of 'movie', so that the tuple $\Omega = (e, a, s, h)$ would look like this, as 'scared' is typically assigned negative sentiment:

$$\Omega_1 = Update(\Omega_1) = (movie, \_, (great, \_, +, 1), speaker).$$

The second sentence, it would originally look like this:

$$\Omega_2 = (movie, \_, (scared, \_, -, 1), speaker)$$

However, this second sentence needs to be updated three times: first, the adjective 'scared' is modified by the adverb 'so' (negative sentiment is intensified); then, discourse-level features are applied and it is understood that the first sentence indicates that the whole is positive; and finally a third update of pragmatic nature takes place, which indicates an additional positive evaluation. This process would proceed as follows:

Ω_2 = Update sentence(Ω_2) = (movie, _, (so scared, _, --,2), speaker).
Ω_2 = Update discourse(Ω_2) = (movie, _, (so scared, _,+,2), speaker).
Ω_2 = Update pragma(Ω_2) = (movie, _, {(so scared, _,+,2), (didn't move...seat, _,+,2)},speaker).

This model is eminently descriptive and theoretical, so it anticipates future work on sentiment analysis. The authors propose two directions of exploration to improve the knowledge of different contexts: (a) increasing the lexicon so that more contextual information is available and (b) combining different linguistic theories with a mainly quantitative approach to data analysis. In this way, new insights can be gained which, in turn, would improve the efficiency of sentiment analysis systems.

6 Sentiment analysis

6.1 Definition and applications

Liu (2012) defines *sentiment analysis* as a Natural Language Processing task that studies the opinions, sentiments, evaluations, attitudes, and emotions of individuals or an audience in relation to different entities and their attributes that are expressed in written texts.

Although the term appeared only at the beginning of the 21st century, there were earlier studies proposing computational models related to opinion, sentiment adjectives or subjectivity analysis. Dovring (1954) documents the use of textual analysis techniques in 18th century Sweden, when censorship examinations were conducted by searching for lexical selections in religious hymns that were potentially threatening to the morals of the time. In the early 1960s, the General Inquirer research group initiated a project to compile a multi-category list of words for use in psychosociological research. This list (Stone/Hunt 1963) is still employed in a variety of natural language processing applications, including sentiment analysis.

With the advent of the Web 2.0 and the subsequent generation of large amounts of text of all kinds, the term *sentiment analysis* began to acquire its own specific definition in various statistical studies at the beginning of the 21st century. This was also likely the first NLP-related working paper to attempt to assign semantic orientation to particular topics or aspects in text. In parallel, the term *opinion mining* appeared with very much the same meaning in the paper 'Mining the peanut gallery: Opinion extraction and semantic classification of product reviews' by Dave/Lawrence/Pennock (2003), which dealt with the identification of the unique properties of various texts extracted from the web for the automatic detection of positive and negative reviews. Other names for the discipline have been *rating extraction* or *review mining* (Pang/Lee 2008).

The study of public opinion has always been a point of interest, especially since the popularity of market studies carried out from the second half of the 20th century onwards. Due to the rise of the Internet in the 21st century, the number and types of information resources are growing exponentially. As a result, humans face the challenge of transforming this wealth of information to develop disciplines with new visions and perspectives. Even today, the European Central Bank's[4] demand for opinions and the evaluation of political leaders are conducted by traditional polls, funded by organizations that conduct routine or on-demand surveys. Only a small percentage of these datasets are ultimately accessible to the general public, and their methods of data analysis are opaque in many instances. A notorious example of such type of data collection is the Monthly Michigan Index of Consumer Sentiment which provides insight into the confidence and attitudes of American consumers regarding the economy (Batra/Rao 2010; Yu/Duan/Cao 2013).

Regarding the use of the terms *sentiment* and *opinion*, there are subtle differences as they coincide semantically in many aspects. While an *opinion* refers to a person's concrete and rational view, *sentiment* falls within the realm of emotions. Liu (2015) illustrates this difference in a simple way: 'I am worried about the country's economic situation' as opposed to 'I think the country's economy is going badly'. In the former we might reply 'I share your sentiment' while in the latter we would typically reply 'I (dis)agree with you.' Utterances expressing sentiment or opinion include words of a subjective nature, as opposed to objective utterances that include data or facts. Likewise, such objective expressions may also include positive or negative sentiment, by indicating desirable or undesirable facts. As a discipline, sentiment analysis has

---

4   The European Money and Finance Forum, Banca d'Italia, the ECB and the European Investment Bank hosted a joint conference on "The use of surveys for monetary and economic policy" in April 2023. https://www.ecb.europa.eu/pub/conferences/html/20230502-surveys-for-monetary-economic-policy-CALL.en.html

focused on detecting opinions and identifying their polarity so that text segments that convey positive or negative sentiment can be quantified.

Sentiment analysis focuses on extracting information about attitudes from the analysis of text documents of varying length and origin, especially from social networks. Compared to other related fields, such as affective computing, the target problems are approached in a more direct and effective way, since no methods of complete understanding of texts are proposed. Documents are treated as lexical sets that include semantic features – a positive or negative polarity – based on the presence or absence of certain lexical items, grammatical patterns, or other text elements (e.g., punctuation marks, emoticons). Although some systems include within this set emotion detection (e.g., Toret Medina 2015), which attempts to classify utterances as belonging to one or more emotions (such as joy, anger, sadness, disgust), typical sentiment analysis systems do not tackle this task. The result of sentiment analysis is usually a classification of documents on a sentiment scale, from negative to positive (Waloszek/Waloszek 2017). In terms of natural language understanding, sentiment analysis can be recognized as a sub-area of semantic analysis, as sentiment, or *semantic orientation*, is a part of the meaning of utterances.

The range of application domains is very wide. Virtually any entity that can be rated (products, services, or even individuals and organizations) is liable to be analyzed in terms of sentiment, from movies (e.g., Pang/Lee/Vaithyanathan 2002), books (e.g., Srujan et al. 2018) hotels (e.g., Moreno-Ortiz/Pineda Castillo/Hidalgo García 2010) or assessing investor attitudes (Bollen/Mao/Zeng 2011). Likewise, sentiment analysis has been applied to the study of political debate (Wang et al. 2012) or in order to predict election results based on comments made by users online (Tumitan/Becker 2014). Other fields of application have been political discourse (Gallardo Paúls 2017), journalistic analysis (Godbole/Srinivasaiah/Skiena 2007), legal (Garofalo 2017), psychology (Tao et al. 2016) or education (Fernández-Cruz 2017).

As we saw in section 5.1, within the sentiment quintuple (e, a, s, h, t) (Liu 2015), sentiment (s) is the central and essential element for any kind of sentiment analysis; the rest of the elements (entity, aspect, opinion holder, time) may or may not be relevant depending on the needs and scope of the analysis and the possibilities offered by the different systems. On the other hand, these systems can be described according to a number of variables:

1. Interest: although sentiment analysis started as an NLP task with the clear practical aim of automatically classifying online opinions of products and services, and therefore with obvious commercial intentions, linguistic and social studies have benefitted enormously from the technical developments, as they facilitate acquiring quantitative and qualitative insights from texts.
2. Granularity: sentiment analysis systems have several levels of detail when analyzing texts: document, sentence and aspect. We provide further details on this in section 6.2.
3. Approaches: roughly speaking, machine learning and lexicon-based approaches are employed. The two can be, and often are, combined (hybrid approaches).
4. Scale: the result can be expressed as either a binary classification (often referred to as thumbs up/ thumbs down), a three-point scale (positive, neutral, negative) or a multi-point scale that mimics the now pervasive star-rating system, often referred to a as seeing stars (Pang/Lee 2005).

Liu (2015) states that the key to successful sentiment classification is effective feature engineering, something that is common to all machine-learning based systems. In the case of sentiment analysis, the most salient are the following:

- Terms and frequency: these are individual words (unigrams) and their n-grams associated with frequency counts, essentially what is called a *bag-of-words*. These are the features most commonly used in traditional text classification (topic identification).
- Part of speech: the proportion of adjectives usually determines the level of subjectivity of a text. In descending order, adverbs, nouns and verbs are the also important sentiment indicators.
- Sentiment-laden words and phrases: in addition to individual words, there are idioms and other types of multi-word expressions, such as 'cost somebody an arm and a leg', whose semantic orientation needs to be accounted for in order to calculate overall sentiment.

- Sentiment shifters: in addition to sentiment words and phrases, other language constructs can be used to express sentiment or modify their orientation or intensity, such as negatives, modals, intensifiers, and hedges.
- Semantic dependency: certain grammatical structures may determine a particular expression of sentiment.

6.2 Classification levels

Sentiment classification can be carried out at three different levels; in increasing order of complexity these are document, sentence, and aspect-level.

6.2.1 Document-level sentiment classification

Document-level sentiment classification is considered the simplest task of sentiment analysis. It simply classifies a document as positive or negative or places it on a scale of higher granularity. In this type of analysis it is not necessary to detect entities or aspects.

There is a wide range of classification algorithms that can perform, among others, sentiment analysis tasks. An example of this would be classification across different languages and/or different language domains. Typically, these classifiers have been implemented using preclassified texts as training data, such as reviews of a single product, because only a single entity is evaluated. This method is not recommended for use with, for instance, Internet forum discussions, interviews, or news articles, as they frequently combine multiple entities. Even if, given a prior classification, it is certain that a document exclusively evaluates a single entity, this type of system will provide a single generalized sentiment score.

A translation of this problem into formal terms, according to the model described in section 6.1 would be the following: document-level sentiment classification assumes that an opinion document d expresses sentiment *s* about a general entity *e* and that it only contains opinions from a single opinion sender *h*. As we mentioned, in this level of analysis sentiment *s* would be assigned to a GENERAL aspect within the opinion quintuple. As for the entity, opinion holder and time are assumed to be unknown or irrelevant to the study.

6.2.2 Sentence-level sentiment classification

Document-level sentiment classification provides results with low level of detail relative to the requirements of some practical applications. For example, when different opinion objects (targets) are referred to in a document, it is necessary to obtain greater levels of detail beyond the document level. Sentence-level classification is an intermediate step in the overall sentiment analysis task and does not take into consideration several elements of the sentiment analysis quintuple: entity and aspect detection, opinion holder or time. Thus the sentence-level classification problem is formally formulated as 'given a sentence x, determine whether x expresses a positive, negative or neutral (or no) opinion' (Liu 2015: 70). For practical purposes, most sentences express a single sentiment so most sentiment analysis tasks do not need to determine the aspect of entities, nor the opinion sender and, moreover, these elements are easy to detect by prior textual classification techniques.

As is the case in this study, it is possible to conduct document-level analysis on one-sentence documents using sentence-level sentiment analysis. However, according to Liu (2012), this task is more difficult because the information contained in a single sentence is much shorter than the information contained in a typical document containing multiple sentences. Numerous systems that perform classification at this level have trouble accurately classifying sentiment into three basic classes (positive, negative, and neutral) and frequently bypass the classification of neutral sentences, with a tendency to positivize or negatively punctuate them. However, this cannot be ignored, as a document may contain numerous sentences that do not express emotion, as a neutral result typically, but not exclusively, denotes factuality or absence of emotion.

Although they share a line of demarcation, sentiment and subjectivity are not synonymous. Subjectivity is a key term that has been widely employed in sentiment analysis at the sentence level, and its application is frequently a source of confusion. Consideration of a sentence's subjectivity and the assumption that it contains a sentiment load were conceptually equivalent in a number of publications. However, these are not equivalent concepts. Therefore, it is necessary to reiterate that a sentence will be defined as subjective when it originates from an individual's mental perspective rather than from a verifiable experience stemming from physical world experience. Consequently, while an objective sentence conveys information in a factual manner, a subjective sentence expresses personal feelings, opinions, or beliefs. Subjectivity classification is the process of identifying whether a sentence is objective or subjective (Riloff/Wiebe 2003).

It should be noted that subjective expressions related to sentiment express appreciation, evaluation, desire, belief, suspicion, speculation, etc. (Wiebe 2000). As a counterpoint, it should be noted that there are subjective sentences that do not contain opinion or sentiment. Moreover, objective sentences may imply opinions or sentiments caused by desirable or undesirable facts. For example:

(4) Floor collapses at Jakarta stock exchange, dozens injured.[5]

Therefore, Liu (2015) proposes distinguishing between *opinionated* (if it implies a positive or negative sentiment) and *non-opinionated*.

Considering these factors, the classification at sentence level is carried out by solving two problems, first subjectivity identification, i.e., whether a sentence expresses an opinion or not, and then classification of sentiment itself. Among the practical implementations, there are several models based on machine learning or lexicon, notably those proposed by Wiebe/Bruce/O'Hara (1999) or Riloff/Wiebe (2003), which offer subjective perspectives based on presumptive syntactic patterns.

On the other hand, a system for analyzing sentiment at the sentence level assumes that each sentence contains a single expression of sentiment. This assumption, however, works well for simple sentences (subject-verb-object) with a single sentiment, but it is not appropriate for those that include several opinions, for example in comparative or concessive sentences. When a sentence contains multiple sentiments, it

---

5 https://edition.cnn.com/2018/01/15/asia/jakarta-stock-exchange-intl/index.html

can be assigned the MIXED wildcard class (Liu, 2015). Also, a general positive or negative tone should be detected, but it may obviate details, for example in the following sentence:

(5) HSBC keeps increasing dividends despite regulatory uncertainties.

Sentence-level ranking can only be applied to sentences expressing opinions of a common nature but cannot be applied to sentences expressing comparative opinions. The sentence in (6) expresses sentiment in a clear manner, however, it is not possible to classify it effectively through a single positive, negative or neutral score.

(6) A reloadable debit card works better than a bank account.

To conclude, sentence-level sentiment classification comes closer to solving the problem of relating opinion targets to their sentiment with finer granularity than document-level classification. However, its practical application has a number of limitations. Although a generalization can be made using the sentiment of opinion targets, it is extremely difficult to assign a single sentiment score to sentences that mention multiple entities, such as comparisons.

6.2.3 Aspect-level sentiment classification

In a document, such as a user review, there may be more than one entity, topic, or aspect being evaluated. The underlying rationale for this method is that a negative rating of a document does not necessarily imply that the message is pessimistic with regard to all entities or all aspects of the entities being evaluated. An entity is any of the objects, people, phenomena, or events about which we wish to automatically determine their sentiment (Liu, 2015). In different application domains, aspect-based sentiment analysis is referred to by other names, such as topic-based sentiment analysis or entity-based sentiment analysis.

An *entity category* represents an entity with a unique name for use by the sentiment classifier, e.g., RESTAURANT. This category can be referred to by means of different *entity expressions* or *mentions* using near-synonyms or type-of specifications. For example, the entity category RESTAURANT would include the entity expressions 'fast food restaurant' or 'pizza joint'. The process of grouping entity expressions into entity categories is called *entity resolution* or *entity grouping*. Identifying aspects entails the same kind of issues, as they can be referred to by multiple words and phrases. For example, *frame rate* and *resolution* refer to the same aspect (VIDEO) for video cameras. Also, the process of grouping aspect expressions into aspect categories is called *aspect resolution* or *aspect grouping* (Henríquez-Miranda/Guzmán-Luna 2016).

Aspect expressions are usually nouns or noun phrases, but can also be verb phrases, adjectives, adverbs, and other constructions. *Explicit aspect expressions* are aspect expressions that appear overtly in the text as a noun or noun phrase. Many implicit aspect expressions are adjectives or adverbs that qualify or describe specific aspect categories. For example, the aspect 'image quality' of the entity CAMERA in (7). *Implicit aspect expressions* are those that are not of the noun phrase type. Their detection is often a challenge when developing an implementation or even extracting manually.

(7) The image quality of this camera is great.

Based on the previous discussion, it is possible to define an entity model and an opinion model as established by Liu (2011) and summarize the main tasks of the discipline of aspect-based sentiment analysis:

A model of entity is an entity e that is represented in absolute terms and contains a finite set of aspects $A=\{a_1, a_2, a_3, \ldots, a_n\}$ such that e can be expressed textually through a finite set of entity expressions $\{ee_1, ee_2, \ldots, ee_s\}$. Each aspect can be expressed by any of the elements of a finite set of its aspect expressions $\{ae_1, ae_2, \ldots, ae_m\}$.

A model of opinion document is defined as a document d containing opinions of a finite set of entities $\{e_1, e_2, e_3, \ldots, e_r\}$ and each entity includes a subset of aspects. Each of the opinions will be part of a finite set of opinion holders $\{h_1, h_2, h_3, \ldots, h_p\}$ that take place at a given time t.

Given the above definitions, a sentiment analysis system performs at least the following tasks:

1. Entity extraction and its resolution: extract all entity expressions in a document D, and group synonymous expressions under a single entity.

2. Aspect extraction and its resolution: extract all aspect expressions from each of the entities and group synonymous expressions.
3. Opinion holder extraction and resolution: resolve who the opinion holder of each of the opinions is and group their different expressions.
4. Time extraction: extract the time of publication of each publication and normalize the time format.
5. Sentiment classification: classify the sentiment expressed in D on rating scale.
6. Opinion quintuple generation: produce all opinion quintuples (e, a, s, h, t) expressed in D based on the results of the previous tasks.

Performing this set of tasks is a highly complex process that requires sophisticated sentiment classifiers that combine various techniques. Furthermore, two additional tasks analogous to the second task are contemplated (Liu 2015):

- Opinion reason: extract the reason expressions for each opinion and group them into clusters.
- Opinion qualifier: extract qualifier expressions for each opinion and group them into clusters.

Aspect-level sentiment classification also involves multiple ways of implementation (e.g., through machine learning, syntax or ontologies) and presents a number of problems. Determining the entity as well as the scope of each sentiment expression is a challenging task. For example, in (8) the scope of application of the sentiment word 'bad' covers only 'economy', but not 'Apple'.

(8) Apple is doing very well in this bad economy.

Boiy/Moens (2009) approach proposes to compute the weight of each of the features by calculating the distance between the word representing the entity or aspect and the related opinion object. Other authors, such as Cadilhac/Benamara/Aussenac-Gilles (2010), Freitas/Vieira (2013) and Lau/Li/Liao (2014), propose to use ontologies to define the relevant entities and aspects, give them structure, and define application constraints. For example, when the opinion is expressed about a specific feature of the object, then it is clearly understood that this sentiment is specific to the object and not to the whole. This is illustrated by (9) where the entity 'Greece' has the attribute 'economic figures'. The negative sentiment is not directed at the whole of Greece, only at its economy.

(9) Greece's economic figures are terrible.

Aspect-level sentiment analysis is therefore the most complex level of analysis, as it includes in its analysis all opinion-related variables. In practice, however, most problems do not need to identify each and every of the elements of the quintuple to perform efficient sentiment analysis since some of them may be not present in the text, pragmatically implicit or simply irrelevant.

6.3 Machine learning approaches to sentiment analysis

Machine learning methods employ learning algorithms that are trained on labeled data to obtain a predictive model that is later able to classify unseen examples. Thus, these systems are fully dependent on the availability of 'training' data from which to learn. But training a classifier is in itself a complex process that consists of several steps:

1. Problem definition: where the specific scope of the task is defined. This could be a binary sentiment classification (positive/negative), a multi-class sentiment classification (positive/negative/neutral), or a regression problem (to predict a score on a scale).
2. Data collection: gather data relevant to the problem at hand. Social media posts, customer reviews, tweets, etc. have traditionally been used, especially those for which a numerical or categorical score is available, and there is no need to manually label the examples. The dataset should ideally be large and diverse enough to capture the different ways sentiment can be expressed in the domain.

3. Data preprocessing: text data usually needs a good amount of cleaning and preprocessing. This could include lowercasing, punctuation removal, tokenization, stop word removal, stemming or lemmatization, etc. The goal is to convert the raw text into a form that can be understood by a machine learning model.
4. Feature extraction: convert the cleaned text into numerical features that can be used as input for the model. The most basic feature extraction techniques are the bag-of-words approach and TF-IDF. More sophisticated approaches include pre-trained word embeddings like Word2Vec (Mikolov et al. 2013) or Transformers-based models like BERT (Devlin et al. 2019).
5. Model training:this is where the actual learning takes place and the predictive model is generated, based on the selected features and the labeled data. Classical machine learning algorithms include Naive Bayes, decision trees and Support Vector Machines. Currently, learning models based on neural networks constitute the state of the art, specifically Transformer-based models have improved on both Convolutional Neural Networks (CNNs), Recurrent Neural Networks (RNNs), including Long Short-Term Memory (LSTM) networks.
6. Evaluation: the predictive model needs to be formally evaluated in terms of performance, for which a separate validation set is employed, using appropriate metrics like accuracy, precision, recall, F1-score, or ROC-AUC.
7. Hyperparameter tuning: the resulting predictive model can be finetuned by modifying some of the learning parameters.

Once created, the predictive model can be used to classify unseen documents. It is important to understand that the performance indicated by the evaluation metrics is only to be expected with the same type of texts that the model was trained on. Although there have been numerous initiatives to adapt existing models to new domains (different than the one they were trained on), this is still a major disadvantage of machine learning systems, and the one directly responsible for the 'bias issue' that current artificial intelligence is often faulted for.

Currently, Transformers-based systems have proved to have the strongest performance across a number natural language processing tasks (including sentiment analysis) and a variety of benchmarks. The most salient Transformers-based systems are the following:

- BERT (Bidirectional Encoder Representations from Transformers) (Devlin et al. 2019). Developed by Google, BERT is pre-trained on a large corpus of text data and is then fine-tuned for specific tasks like sentiment analysis. BERT was the first Transformers system, characterized by its bidirectional training, which allows it to have a deeper sense of language context and flow than previous, single-direction language models.
- RoBERTa (Robustly Optimized BERT Pretraining Approach) (Liu et al. 2019). RoBERTa is a variant of BERT developed by Facebook. It builds on BERT by adjusting key hyperparameters, removing the next-sentence pretraining objective, and training with much larger mini-batches and learning rates. The result is a model that achieves comparable performance to BERT but is simpler and more efficient to train, making it a good choice for sentiment analysis. Many fine-tuned models for sentiment analysis based on Roberta have been generated and made available to the public, which makes them a popular 'of-the-shelf' option for classification of frequent document types such as tweets and user reviews.
- DistilBERT (Sanh et al. 2019) is a smaller, faster, cheaper and lighter version of BERT developed by HuggingFace. It retains over 95 % of BERT's performance while being twice as fast, making it well-suited for sentiment analysis tasks where computational resources or time are constraints.
- XLNet (Yang et al. 2019) is a generalized autoregressive pretraining method that outperforms BERT on several NLP benchmarks. It captures the bidirectional context by maximizing the expected likelihood over all permutations of the factorization order and overcomes the limitations of BERT due to its autoregressive formulation.
- GPT (Generative Pretrained Transformer) (Brown et al. 2020). Developed by OpenAI, GPT is primarily a language generation model, but it can also be fine-tuned for classification tasks like sentiment analysis. The current version, GPT-4, has demonstrated

a remarkable ability to understand context, making it suitable for highly sophisticated language understanding and generation tasks. At the time of writing, GPT, popularized by the well-known ChatGPT application, is undoubtedly the most well-known language model, having transcended the scientific realm and reached massive popularity among the general public.

Machine learning methods have been shown repeatedly to outperform supervised, lexicon-based approaches (Maas et al. 2011; Socher et al. 2013; Zhang/Wang/Liu 2018), which we describe in the following section. However, this is true only if we reduce sentiment analysis to a text classification task, which is the prevailing perspective. However, lexicon-based systems are advantageous to the language researcher, as they are able to provide insights by identifying sentiment-laden words and phrases that can then be studied in context.

Lexicon-based sentiment analysis systems offer a crucial further advantage: they do not need to be trained for specific domains (although some systems do permit the use of specific-domain lexicons). Finally, many machine-learning sentiment analysis systems have been shown to have performance when combined with sentiment dictionaries.

6.4 Lexicon-based sentiment analysis

Lexicon-based sentiment analysis relies on a sentiment dictionary, i.e., a collection of precompiled sentiment terms. A sentiment lexicon usually has the form of a database, that is, a list of words and multi-word units and their polarity (positive, negative, or neutral), and possibly their intensity and other data, such as part of speech. For example, the adjective 'happy' could be categorized as positive and assigned a score of +3, while 'sad' could be categorized as negative and assigned a score of −3. The sentiment of a text is determined as a function of the combined sentiment of its lexical items. The function can be as simple as a count of positive and negative words in a text, with the difference between the two counts determining the overall tone. The text is classified as positive if it contains more positive words than negative ones, and vice versa.

Therefore, the quality and coverage of the sentiment dictionary of a lexicon-based system is key to its performance. However, it is important to note that context and subject domain play a very important role, as they can modify the initial (i.e., dictionary) sentiment of words and phrases. This refers both to the immediate (i.e., sentence-level) context, and wider, more abstract context (i.e., discourse level). For instance, at the sentence level, the word 'small' may invert its polarity when preceded by the modifier 'not', and, can be negative when describing a hotel room, but positive when describing a laptop computer.

As we have discussed in section 6.3, machine learning techniques usually perform better in the specialized domains for which they are trained, but domain specificity can also be accounted for by lexicon-based systems. The former, however, are unable to provide cues or insights into the text, which the latter can. Immediate context, on the other hand, also requires special treatment in the case of lexicon-based systems, as a simple negative adverb can radically alter the semantic orientation of a sentiment word.

After many years of sentiment analysis research and development, many sentiment dictionaries exist and are available for research and commercial purposes; we review these in section 6.4.2. However, semi-automatic ways to generate both general and specific-domain sentiment lexicons have been described in the literature.

6.4.1 Sentiment lexicon generation

Over the years, researchers have compiled sentiment dictionaries using different approaches, fundamentally from existing dictionaries, such as thesauri, and from corpora. In the dictionary-based approach, new sentiment words are extracted by leveraging their semantic relationships to a small set of hand-picked opinion words, known as the *seed set*, from which related words, potentially sharing the same polarity (or the opposite) are identified. Examples of this approach are Kim/Hovy (2004), Kamps et al. (2004) and Godbole/Srinivasaiah/Skiena (2007). The effectiveness of this method depends on the quantity and quality of relationships in the synonym and antonym entries in the dictionary used.

These methods often produce flawed lexicons, but it is straightforward to perform manual proofreading to correct them.

The second approach to sentiment lexicon generation utilizes corpora instead of dictionaries. In this approach, a seed set is also used to then automatically discover other words that occur in similar contexts. For example, Hatzivassiloglou/McKeown (1997) identified sentiment words using patterns that made use of conjunctions in a corpus of 21 million words from the Wall Street Journal, and generated a lexicon from a list of seed adjectives. They considered that two adjectives separated by a copulative conjunction (e.g., ADJ + 'and' + ADJ) must have the same polarity, and, inversely, adjectives separated by an adversative conjunction (ADJ + 'but' + ADJ) should be assigned the opposite polarity. Turney (2002) combined a number of information retrieval techniques and pointwise mutual information (PMI) to identify sentence polarity. Although this method is not designed to develop a sentiment lexicon, it allows the identification of the potential polarity of sentiment words in the documents being classified. PMI is a statistical technique that can be used to measure the match between two words or phrases. Thus, the polarity of a word will be the difference of its PMI with a positive word and with a negative word. The two keywords chosen by the author are 'excellent' and 'poor', which are considered to be the most commonly used in online reviews.

6.4.2 Available sentiment lexicons

A number of lexicons have been produced and are available for research purposes with some limitations. In this section, the describe some of the most salient general-purpose lexicons, as we will tackle financial-economic domain-specific ones in section 6.5.1.

The *General Inquirer* (Stone/Hunt 1963) is one of the oldest and most popular sentiment lexicons. It was motivated by a study in cognitive psychology and content analysis. Easily accessible on the Internet, it is used in a large number of papers. It provides syntactic, semantic and pragmatic information. Sentiment classification of lexical items is based on 182 categories, mainly: positive, negative, strong, weak, active, pleasure or pain. It includes 1915 positive and 2291 negative items.

Hu/Liu's (2004) *Opinion Lexicon* collects approximately 6,800 words extracted from product reviews, originally labeled by bootstrapping part of the WordNet adjectival sets of synonyms and antonyms. It contains 2,006 positive and 4,783 negative units.

Wilson et al.'s (2005) *Multiperspective Question Answering Subjectivity Lexicon* (MPQA) includes 2,718 positive and 4,912 negative lexical units. They were extracted from a number of sources, including the General Inquirer, Hatzivassiloglou and McKeown's (1997) word list, and the list of subjective cues obtained by applying bootstrapping techniques (Riloff/Wiebe 2003). This lexicon was hand-labeled and includes four polarity categories (positive, negative, neutral, and both) and a subjectivity level label. Most words are classified as negative (33.1 %) or positive (59.7 %), while a small number (0.3 %) are annotated with both polarities, and 6.9 % as neutral.

SentiWordNet 3.0 (Baccianella/Esuli/Sebastiani 2010) is not a mere lexicon, but a sentiment ontology. It is designed from the statistical annotation of the hierarchical structure of WordNet 3.0, whose entries were assigned positive, negative or neutral values. In its latest version the annotation algorithm has refined its scores by applying massive random walk statistical strategies together with semi-supervised learning.

The *Macquarie Semantic Orientation Lexicon* (MSOL) (Mohammad/Dunne/Dorr 2009) includes about 76,400 lexical items (51,208 words and 25,192 multiword expressions) labeled as positive or negative in a semi-automatic way. It was compiled from a seed lexicon and an algorithm that labeled entries from a Roget-type thesaurus. It includes 30,458 positive and 45,942 negative units.

The *NRC Emotion lexicon/EmoLex* (Mohammad/Turney 2010) is a lexicon that, in addition to sentiment, categorizes words according to eight basic emotions (anger, fear, anticipation, confidence, surprise, sadness, joy, and disgust). Its 14,182 entries were manually tagged via crowdsourcing on the Amazon Mechanical Turk platform.

The *Sentiment140 Lexicon* (Mohammad/Kiritchenko/Zhu 2013) was created from a collection of 1.6 million tweets. It includes 62,468 unigrams, 677,698 bigrams, and 480,010 pairs labeled as positive or negative.

LIWC2015 (Pennebaker et al. 2015) is part of the LIWC software and only available through this application. It includes 6,400 entries (words, stems, etc.) and additionally classifies words according to their syntactic and psychological features.

VADER (*Valence Aware Dictionary and sEntiment Reasoner*) (Hutto/Gilbert 2014) is a lexicon containing 7,500 entries (lexicon, emoticons and Internet slang) and focuses on the study of sentiment in social networks based on a manual review performed through Amazon Mechanical Turk.

Lingmotif-Lex (Moreno-Ortiz/Pérez-Hernandez 2018) is the basis of Lingmotif and has several main components: the lexicon that includes simple lexical units, multiword expressions and emojis, and a set of contextual rules. It is labeled according to sentiment (positive, negative, and neutral) and intensity (in the range 1–3).

6.4.3 Contextual valence shifters

The calculation of the polarity of a text or sentence depends not only on the presence of sentiment words and phrases, but also on other elements such as negative particles or the use of intensifiers and diminishers. With a view to implementing a system to deal with this problem, Polanyi/Zaenen (2006) proposed at a theoretical level what they called *sentiment shifters* or *contextual valence shifters*, a series of rules that modify the initial sentiment of lexical items by means of inversion, intensification or attenuation. Researchers have implemented these in multiple ways. For example, in Hu/Liu's (2004) and Kim/Hovy's (2004) systems, each positive sentiment expression is assigned the value of +1 and each negative sentiment expression is assigned the value −1. In this model, negation words, such as 'not' or 'never', reverse the semantic orientation of the sentiment words they modify. Other pioneers in its technical implementation were Kennedy/Inkpen (2006) and, in Spanish, Moreno-Ortiz et al.'s (2013), whose context rules system was first implemented in Sentitext (Moreno-Ortiz/Pérez Pozo/Torres Sánchez 2010) and later in Lingmotif (Moreno-Ortiz 2016). Their model implements a classifier of contextual values in text of three types: negation, intensifiers and attenuators.

The paradigmatic model in the English language is the Sentiment Orientation Calculator (SO-CAL) by Taboada et al. (2011) who extended the previous model and proposed a more refined approach that deserves a closer look. In this system, the sentiment score of each item moves in a range [-5, +5]. In this system, the intensification or attenuation of sentiment-laden units works as follows (a) when an adjective with a positive or negative sentiment label occurs next to a modifying adverb (e.g., 'very good') or (b) when a noun with a sentiment label is modified by an adjective annotated as an intensifier or attenuator (e.g., 'total failure'). The effect of intensifiers and attenuators works from a linear system of addition and subtraction. This series of intensifiers or attenuators are annotated with a certain percentage weight. For example, the particle 'slightly' is assigned −50 % in relation to the score of the noun it precedes, 'somewhat' −30 %, 'pretty' −10 %, 'really' adds 15 %, 'very' +25 % and 'extremely' +90 %, and so on. In the case where these items are chained, they are applied recursively by taking as a starting point the lexical unit closest to the sentiment word (e.g., 'most excellent'). In this way, the sentiment 'really very good' would be modelled more efficiently from multiplications, rather than through additions, as follows [3 * [100 % + 25 %]] (Benamara et al. 2012).

The inversion of sentiment orientation is a more problematic task, as there is great difficulty in applying negation rules to a strongly positive word, as, in many cases, it simply attenuates the sentiment. Negation may be realized as affixes, such as 'un-', 'a-', or '-less' or through negative polarity items, such as nouns, adverbs or verbs, or appear only in sentences of a negative nature which have no corresponding in affirmative sentences (Israel 2011). There are several approaches to deal with negation. While Taboada et al. (2011) consider that it determines neutral sentiment (e.g., 'This is not good management'), other authors, such as Benamara et al. (2012) observe that accumulations of negative polarity elements reinforce sentiments within their scope (e.g., 'There is no lack of liquidity in the US economy' would be a positive expression). Some studies consider that negation in the sentence is much more marked than affirmation from its own psychological essence (Osgood/Richards 1973), despite the fact that negative expressions are usually presented cushioned by rhetorical resources of a positive nature. Thus, Taboada et al. (2011) proposed that negative sentiment expressions weigh more when calculating sentiment automatically.

Other contextual factors to be taken into account are mood and modality. These aspects of meaning provide information within the sentence that transcends its propositional content. Adverbials indicating evidentiality ('perhaps', 'maybe'), conditionals, modals ('could', 'may'), and multiword expressions acting as modals ('a possibility is...', 'we consider that...').

Irrealis moods, in particular, present certain implementation difficulties, as it is not straightforward to determine the implied sentiment. To this end, Brooke/Tofiloski/Taboada (2009) propose to ignore this type of propositions, a strategy they called *irrealis blocking*. Benamara et al. (2017) consider that there are some cases that need to be studied carefully, since it is possible to structure rules that compute the sentiment of cumulative modality from the local grammar. However, there are not many studies describing the relationship of these modality patterns, nor the contextual modification of sentiment values.

In addition to those cited above, a practical implementation is found in Liu's (2010) *opinion rules*, later called *sentiment composition rules* (2015). They are primarily used to modify sentiment scoring in a lexicon-based system, although they can also be used as effective features, many of them manually labeled, in supervised learning.

6.5 Domain-specific sentiment classification

In an early discussion of semantic search, Hampp/Lang (2005) discussed the feasibility of adapting a lexicon to specific industries, such as manufacturing, services, or government, in order to take full advantage of the ability to detect particularities and understand the sentiment associated with those words. They suggest that domain-specific knowledge can be leveraged to facilitate the disambiguation of terms and better understand the context. As reiterated throughout this work, sentiment classification is very sensitive to specific domains.

When studying the sentiment of specialized languages in sentiment analysis, two questions arise, (a) which factors have the most weight in determining the sentiment of a text; and (b) are there positive or negative words related to a particular domain that do not have the same polarity in general language or other domains? Classifiers trained with domain-specific datasets often obtain higher accuracy than lexicon-based method precisely because they identify sentiment words automatically in that particular domain. It is for this reason that in lexicon-based systems a domain adaptation becomes necessary. Therefore, an in-depth study of the domain is necessary to establish relevant strategies when studying sentiment in an automated way (Liu 2015; Malo et al. 2014; Moreno-Ortiz/Fernández-Cruz 2015; Moreno-Ortiz/Fernandez-Cruz/Pérez-Hernández 2020).

One of the first studies to tackle this problem was the one by Aue/Gamon (2005), who proposed a domain transfer strategy in order to tackle the lack of existing labeled data in a new domain. Thus, they experimented with four strategies:

1. Training a mix of existing labeled reviews for other domains and test them on the target domain.
2. Training a classifier as in the first strategy, but limiting it to features observed in the target domain.
3. Using sets of domain classifiers with data that have been previously labeled and test them on the target domain.
4. Combining small amounts of labeled data with large amounts of unlabeled data from the target domain (this is the traditional semi-supervised learning setting).

Among the most frequent problems, it is worth mentioning that even within the same domain many words may express different semantic orientations depending on the analyzed entity. According to Liu (2012), these situations usually occur with quantity adjectives (e.g., 'The battery life is long' vs. 'It takes a long time to focus'). This is why identifying domain-dependent sentiment words and their semantic orientations is sometimes insufficient. Some applications working at the entity level have used relations between aspect and sentiment words and used of tuples such as (content_sentiment_word, aspect) in order to represent opinion contexts, e.g., ('long', 'battery life') (Deng et al. 2018). Algorithms such as Popescu/Etzioni's (2005) propose to start from a global label that refines the sentiment of text elements through gradual sweeps: first from a specific corpus and finally at the entity level.

Lingmotif (Moreno-Ortiz 2017) implements a simple and novel method to integrate domain-specific lexical items (single words and multi-word units). Instead of using only one specific lexicon, it combines two: one general (or *core*) lexicon and one specific to the domain of analysis. When a domain-specific lexicon is selected, the sentiment information contained in it overrides that of the core lexicon, which acts as the default lexical resource for lexical items not present in the specific one.

6.5.1 Economics and sentiment analysis

Sentiment analysis in the domain of economics and finance has been given special attention in the literature. The development of sentiment analysis as a discipline developed during an era of financial uncertainty, so it is no coincidence that many studies in this discipline are aimed at analyzing economic events to establish ways of measuring various factors (financial reports, analysis of speeches by relevant figures, analysis of the economic press, etc.) reliably and accurately. The results of these studies have many advantages over traditional methods as they allow constant, real-time monitoring of indicators through automated analysis of opinions relevant to a given index. Economics is a specialized language, and as such it requires expert judgment to define what kind of polarity a given text has (Krishnamoorthy 2017; Loughran/McDonald 2015, 2016; Malo et al. 2014).

The idea of applying textual analysis to financial markets is not entirely novel and the impact of sentiment on markets is well established (Ederington/Lee 1993; Klein/Prestbo 1974). One important pioneer was Niederhoffer (1971), a veteran academic and hedge fund manager who manually analyzed two decades of New York Times economic headlines. These were assigned to nineteen semantic categories on a good-bad scale determining that markets tend to overreact to negative news. He prophetically proposed the development of computational text analysis techniques to obtain more objective results (Devitt/Ahmad 2007b, 2007a). Sentiment analysis studies in the economic and financial domain emerged in the mid 2000s, and mainly studied their relationship with stock market predictions (e.g., Melvin/Yin 2000), the impact of external information, especially press headlines on financial results (Chan 2001; Poon/Granger 2005), or the sentiment of experts towards different firms and their stocks (O'Hare et al. 2009). The work of Tetlock (2007) is a pioneering study that analyzed an investment strategy based on sentiment analysis, and discussed the drawbacks of using probabilistic methods based on judgements that are difficult to replicate. Loughran/McDonald (2011) developed the first extensive sentiment lexicon in the domain of finance, which they extracted from corporate reports.

Experts in the financial field have differing views on how markets respond to news and how the study of news articles can be incorporated into financial strategies. Among the most prominent is the *Efficient Market Hypothesis*, which considers that new information spreads quickly and influences the flow of investments and prices immediately. Thus, changes in future values will reflect future news (Chan/Chong 2017). This approach started to be challenged from the 1980s onwards by behavioral finance. Today, the accepted view in the capitalist economic process is that, along with other factors, emotions do determine the behavior of investors.

Chan/Chong (2017) provide a review of the historical background of the main antecedents of textual analysis in financial markets. The survey by Klein/Prestbo (1974) shows how a pessimistic financial news report can affect markets, and strongly supports the suggestion that news and markets influence each other. Ederington/Lee (1993) conclude that financial texts, especially press releases, can shed light on market volatility. Engle/Ng (1993) proposed the study of the news impact curve, which provides a mechanism to explain market returns using news. Blood/Philips (1995) analyzed the causal influence of news headlines with the consumer sentiment indicator, presidential popularity and various macroeconomic indicators between 1989 and 1993.

In the expression 'sentiment indicator', the term *sentiment* specifically refers to 'financial sentiment' as 'the expectations of market participants relative to a norm: a bullish (bearish) investor expects to be above (below) average, whatever *average* may be' (Fama 1970; Brown/ Cliff 2004: cited in Van de Kauter/Breesch/Hoste 2015: 4999–5000).

Shiller (2000) discusses the key role played by the media in the economic scenario for stock market movements, which are triggered by these in a sort of self-fulfilling prophecy. This is because investors follow certain publications considered influential and market sentiment is, to some extent, driven by news content. In line with this idea, Tetlock (2007) showed that the number of negative words in the Wall Street Journal's *Abreast of the Market* correlates with stock returns at daily frequency from 1984 to 1999. Building on this research, Garcia (2013) constructed a longitudinal measure of sentiment based on financial news from *The New York Times* from 1905 to 2005, and studied its relationship with financial performance. The long time series shows that news polarity helps predict stock performance on a daily frequency, particularly during recessions.

Generally, the studies that have been conducted on sentiment analysis have not been specifically aimed at studying financial texts in depth, and have focussed on multiple statistical type strategies based on financial forecasts.

6.5.2 Characteristics of the economic-financial domain in relation to sentiment analysis

As we have seen, lexicon-based sentiment analyzers rely on lexical sources, so having a detailed specific lexicon is an essential prerequisite for building an efficient economic sentiment analysis system that takes into account the characteristics and particularities of the specific domain. However, Krishnamoorthy (2017) considers inadequate the prediction of financial text polarity exclusively through domain-specific lexicons. Contrary to most sentiment analysis approaches, in this domain news texts do not always include the explicit sentiment of the author, but generally provide factual opinion reflecting desirable or undesirable facts (Van de Kauter et al. 2015) in a given context.

In economics, variation is more important than absolute values. Therefore, to assess the semantic orientation of an opinion in an economic text, one looks for the future state suggested by the indicators found. Terms that indicate the growth or decline of the indicator to which they discuss are generally considered modifiers (e.g., 'rise' or 'fall'). These are also divided into positive and negative, with positive modifiers signalling a quantitative increase and negative modifiers a decrease in their assigned indicator. A great deal of economic terminology is neutral in nature (e.g., 'sales'), however, it includes a strong semantic orientation when combined with certain verbs and other directional lexical items. Systems that exclusively make use of economic/financial terms are likely to classify sentences as neutral, so it is necessary to supplement the lexicon with a set of *directionality rules* (Musat/Trausan-Matu 2010). This situation involves an added difficulty, as the words that convey this meaning are considered to be from the general domain ('rise', 'escalate', 'decrease'), and they acquire semantic orientation only when co-occur with certain specific terms. While in other domains (e.g., movie reviews) sentiment is often expressed in combinations of adjectives and adverbs, in the economic domain one also needs to determine whether the direction of events is favourable or not, from an economic point of view (e.g., 'sales are decreasing') through combinations of verbs and nouns (Malo et al. 2014).

Furthermore, authors of economic language texts are cautious about expressing negative sentiment directly, and therefore *bag-of-words* approaches to sentiment analysis are often not the most effective to analyze financial language, as the classifier simply contrasts the tally of positive and negative words. On the other hand, it is common to find complex sentences as a psychological strategy to express negative sentiment, so that it is diluted in the prosody of the text (Chan/Chong 2017). In this regard, Loughran/McDonald (2011) determined that 73.8 % of the negative words in the General Inquirer, such as 'tax', 'cost', 'board', or 'vice' are not negative in the economic-financial context.

Several authors (Krishnamoorthy 2017; Malo et. al 2014; Musat/Trausan-Matu 2010) examine objective factors, both lexical and structural, highlighting three categories of words:

1. Performance indicators: *lagging indicators* reflect the results of the activity of a firm or institution: 'market share', 'operating profit', 'operating cost', etc. *Leading indicators*, on the other hand, reflect the firm's possible future performance: 'new stores', 'new customers', 'increase in production capacity', etc. These terms have no sentiment per se and are potentially

positive or potentially negative, since their increase or decrease determines the orientation.
2. Directionality of lagging and leading indicators: this refers to the word or expression (usually verbs and deverbal nouns) that describes the direction of events. For example, 'increase', 'rise', 'skyrocket', 'decrease', 'plummet', 'collapse' mark both the sentiment and intensity of performance indicators. Economic indicators are divided into two subsets: one containing indices that increase when the economy is growing (e.g., 'revenue', 'exports') and one with indices that have a positive development during a period of economic decline (e.g., 'unemployment', 'risk', 'yield'). The former set of indicators is 'positive', while the latter is 'negative'.
3. Multi-word units specific to the domain, including terminology, jargon, and terms used more frequently with a different polarity than in the general domain.

6.5.3 Economic sentiment dictionaries

The studies carried out to determine polarity in texts on economics or finance have been of a very varied nature and with eminently practical objectives. Mainly, they have been carried out to predict stock market movements based on news in the press, social networks or corporate reports of companies. To our knowledge, there are no applications that aim to analyze other phenomena of a discursive or sociological nature related to the impact of the economy on different areas of human life. The main approaches to the study of lexicon-based sentiment analysis rely either on general-language lexicons or domain-specific resources. As the domain of economics is a highly specialized language, the application of the former often misclassifies specialized texts, which impacts the performance of classifiers; the General Inquirer has been one of the most widely used lexicons. Of note here are the systems, described above, by Tetlock/Saar-Tsechansky/MacSkassy (2008) and Tetlock (2007). Engelberg (2008) points out that the General Inquirer's positive word list fails to rank for the financial domain. In fact, the study by Loughran/McDonald (2011) indicates that 75 % of the negative words are not negative in the financial domain. As for domain-specific lexicons, they are generally comprehensive, but require extensive lexicographic work; they are either created from scratch (Loughran/McDonald 2011), used in combination with a general domain lexicon, such as *SentiEcon* (Moreno-Ortiz/Fernández-Cruz/Pérez-Hernández 2020), or adapted from a general lexicon for the economic domain (Van de Kauter et al. 2015).

In this decade, domain-specific lexicon generation methods have been proposed that offer significant improvement in classifier performance. Among these, the most prominent specific lexicons are *LM* (Loughran/McDonald 2016) and the *Financial Polarity Lexicon* (FPL) (Malo et al. 2014). Studies arising from these have obtained considerable improvements in sentiment detection (Li/Wang et al. 2014; Li/Xie et al. 2014; Schumaker/Chen 2009).

Loughran/McDonald (2016) manually created a financial lexicon with six word lists: positive, negative, litigious, uncertainty, strong modal, and weak modal. These terms were present in at least 5 % of the documents in a corpus of 10,000 economic texts. The work of Malo et al. (2014) stands out, as it includes a database of multi-word units that includes domain-specific concepts, an extensive list of verbs and expressions aimed at detecting event direction, and a classification of the potentiality of directionality-dependent terms. The resulting system is capable of detecting directionality of entities using sentence parsing. On the other hand, Van de Kauter et al. (2015) designed a Dutch lexicon from the modification of the *Pattern and Duoman* general-language lexicon (53,209 items), with manual tagging of several lexicons, for a total of 3,187 items; as they point out, the lexicon includes both explicit and implicit or factual language. Oliveira/Cortez/Areal (2016) compiled a sentiment lexicon is designed from a previously labeled corpus of *Stocktwits* messages; subsequently, opinion words were identified based on the strength of association with sentiment classes (bullish and bearish).

Statistical or machine learning-based approaches regularly use bag-of-words or n-grams as features to predict sentiment. Koppel/Shtrimberg (2006) designed a method that related economic texts to annotations of the performance of Standard & Poor's index stocks. The most frequent terms were extracted and their sentiment calculated using the results obtained. They noted that the absence of positive words was notable when the documents reported high stock market values. In similar terms, the model designed by Zhang et al. (2014) used an algorithm that accumulates the sentence scores to provide an overall document-level sentiment. Likewise, other systems predicted movements by, among others, analyzing local grammar in financial texts in various languages (Ahmad/Cheng/Almas 2006; Zhao/Ahmad 2015).

7 Language change and semantic prosody

The objective of this research is to identify words that exhibit changes in meaning across time periods or to pinpoint the words that have undergone the most significant shifts in meaning. The meanings of words constantly change over time, reflecting complex processes within language and society. While linguistic change is continuous, there are periods when it occurs more rapidly (Lyons 1981). Given the English language's global role and the influx of new technological vocabulary, it is reasonable to assume that English is currently undergoing a phase of rapid transformation. The changes can range from significant shifts in core word meanings, such as the evolution of the word 'gay' from 'carefree' to 'homosexual' in the 20th century, to more subtle alterations in cultural connotations (Kutuzov et al. 2018), such as the association of 'Ukraine' with 'war' due to the armed conflicts in the country.

The interest in language change in living languages is not a recent phenomenon; it dates back to the 19th century with scholars like the Neogrammarians and the second Wittgenstein. The study of word meaning over time, specifically in terms of lexical semantics, is commonly referred to as semantic shift or semantic change. The theoretical basis of semantic change can be traced to the pre-structuralist postulates of Bréal (1897) who identified six types of semasiological change, including *pejoration* versus *amelioration*, *restriction* versus *expansion*, *metaphor*, and *metonymy*. In the *pejoration* versus *amelioration* axis, the meaning of a word changes to become more positive or negative.

Geeraerts (1997) highlights several driving forces behind semantic change, namely non-referential meaning and cultural motivation, as it evolves with changing cultural perspectives. Semantic change also involves a psychological process of subjectivization, where the objective meaning of a word in the speaker's voice shifts to a subjective meaning that describes an internal or subjective situation (Provencio Garrigós 2016).

The causes of semantic change can be categorized into linguistic drifts involving slow and regular changes in the central meaning of words, and cultural shifts, involving variations in word associations that are mainly culturally motivated (Hamilton/Leskovec/Jurafsky 2016; Kutuzov et al. 2018). Changes in meaning are influenced by variations in lexical relations: both (a) subtle shifts in usage (e.g., 'actually' being used objectively in the 20th century and now is subsequently used in subjective contexts) and (b) overall shifts in the entire semantic space, where the local neighborhood measure of change examines the alterations in the closest associated words (e.g., collocates) of a given word enabling the observation of changes in its core meaning.

Traugott (2000) emphasizes the extralinguistic causes behind variations in meaning, which encompass material, social, and psychological conditions.

In recent years, computational techniques have emerged as a distinct research methodology to study semantic changes. Various linguistic theories and models, such as Diachronic Prototype Semantics (Geeraerts 1997) and the Invited Inference Theory of Semantic Change (Traugott 1985), have been proposed to explain the rules and regularities in semantic change.

Modern diachronic corpus-assisted language studies are diverse and cover different research communities, including natural language processing, computational linguistics, information retrieval, computer science, and political science. Alessi/Partington (2020) consider that the scarcity of studies in the field can be justified by two factors; first, the instruments and methods necessary to carry out this task involve considerable complexity, and, second, observing changes in the short term is also a challenging endeavor.

The task of discovering semantic shifts from data can be framed formally as follows: from a corpus C, we are given a collection of sub-corpora $\{C_1, C_2, \ldots C_n\}$ that consist of texts created during different time periods $\{T_1, T_2, \ldots T_n\}$ (Kutuzov et al. 2018). In what follows we provide a summary of the most important theoretical approaches to observe semantic change from a lexicon-based standpoint.

7.1 Semantic change, sentiment, and event words

Before we undertake the empirical analysis, which we present in the next chapter, certain key questions need to be addressed. What words set the tone of the discourse of a text? Are there specific terms of the specialized domain with a positive or negative semantic orientation, or are they a totally aseptic and context-independent? If a semantic orientation is present, is this sentiment permanent or does it evolve over time? If it does, can we somehow determine the external factors that cause this sentiment to vary? Words and expressions, belonging to both general and specialized languages can convey sentiment, opinions, and beliefs, which are the core of subjectivity in human language (Liu 2012).

This study attempts to trace the evolution of the semantic orientation of a number of English language terms during a socially significant event – the Global Crisis – over a relatively short interval of time of eight years. In particular, we focus on the study of two types of evolution in semantic orientation, as discussed by Bloomfield (1933) or, more recently, by Traugott/Dasher (2001): *amelioration* and *pejoration*.

According to Moessner (2003), the semantic content of words changes as they become associated with more or less favorable concepts than they used to. In this process, the semantic orientation of a given word may evolve by intensifying its positivity or negativity, or the word may even reverse its polarity completely over a given time span. Thus, the meaning of words change as they become associated with more or less favorable concepts than before. This idea is in relation to the Distributional Hypothesis, as encapsulated by Firth's well-known maxim 'You shall know a word by the company it keeps' (1957), and can be referred to as 'meaning by collocation', whereby meaning is obtained as an abstraction at the syntagmatic level, in contrast to the classical semantic theories.

Variation in semantic orientation is undoubtedly difficult to track exclusively through introspection, but if the 'meaning by collocation' method is followed, corpus linguistics and natural language processing techniques can be applied that facilitate this task by analyzing large amounts of text.

Specifically, we focus on short-term changes in semantic orientation, a field that has received little attention, but one which we believe to be promising, as it facilitates the discovery of new meanings and changes in the semantic orientation of words, and the identification of the underlying ideological trends that originate them. It also offers the possibility to establish relationships with the historical situations that motivate these changes (Cavallin 2012; Cook/Stevenson 2010; Crowley/Bowern 2010).

Our methodology is also based on the concept of *event words*, as posed by Moirand (2007, 2016). We conceive that certain lexical units are initially used with a strictly referential function in a given specialized language, that is, their usage is limited to a superficially aseptic and scientific point of view. Later, as a consequence of following a particular event or situation, they may acquire more semantically-oriented, ideological or politicized connotations, as they become associated with other words that do convey a certain sentiment. For example, lexical units such as 'sovereign debt', or 'recapitalization', which originally had exclusively referential meaning within a specialized domain, have acquired negative connotations as they have repeatedly appeared in negative contexts (related to the economic crisis). Eventually, these words end up acquiring new lexical dimensions according to real-world events, opinions and interpretations produced by both the authorities and the public and, ultimately, the impact that these events exert on the memory of a community of speakers.

7.2 Semantic prosody

Corpus linguistics and natural language processing techniques provide methods and tools that allow to process large amounts of contextualized text with very high levels of precision. Some of these tools are particularly suited to study how different text types evolve over short periods of time (Alessi/Partington 2020), specifically by studying how collocation can modify the orientation of words.

Williams (2001) evidenced the important role played by collocational networks in shaping the meaning of words. The connotations acquired by a word's meaning gradually overshadow its original semantics. Similarly, Hoey (2005) expanded the concept of *lexical priming*, proposing that a word gradually acquires meaning for each individual speaker as it becomes associated with specific collocations, colligations, and semantic and pragmatic associations. Repetition is a crucial factor, as each encounter with a particular word reinforces or alters this conditioning process.

The notion of *semantic prosody* or *semantic association* is very relevant to our analysis. Sinclair (1991) and Louw (1993) introduced this concept, which referred to expressions primarily associated with positive or negative collocates. Louw defined semantic prosody as 'a consistent aura of meaning with which a form is imbued by its collocates' (p. 157), contributing to evaluative harmony and listener comprehension.

Importantly, semantic prosody is not a static property of the lexicon as it varies over time. Bublitz (2003) argues that a set of collocations evolves to acquire a certain sentiment over a specific time period and within a particular context.

One of the challenges of studying semantic prosody is that it is a subjective and context-dependent phenomenon. The evaluative meanings associated with a word or phrase can vary depending on the speaker, the audience, and the situational context. Therefore, it is important to analyze semantic prosody in context and to consider the various factors that can influence its interpretation.

Partington (2004) discusses the concept of semantic prosody in relation to the evaluative meanings conveyed through prosodic elements. Prosodies, while part of the language system, differ from other types of meaning as they are not always consciously activated or perceived. They can be influential in persuasion and practical purposes, often appearing as non-obvious meaning in discourse. Additionally, prosodic meanings are probabilistic, varying in strength and likelihood depending on the item and context. The author also suggests that the quality and strength of prosody can differ across genres or domains, indicating that evaluative meanings may vary based on the communicative context and genre-specific lexicon and grammar.

The concept of *semantic prosody* has, however, faced academic debate. Stubbs (2001) suggests replacing the term with *discourse prosodies* to maintain the distinction between semantics (independent of speakers) and pragmatics (related to speaker attitude) while emphasizing the role of discourse prosodies in creating coherence in discourse. Similarly, in a belligerent paper, Whitsitt (2005) questions the nature of the phenomenon and finding no significant differences from connotation.

Bednarek (2008b) believes that semantic prosody is not straightforward, as collocation with sentiment words does not automatically lead to the acquisition of the same evaluative sense. Another aspect of semantic prosody that she considers that is often overlooked is its multifaceted nature. While many studies have focussed on positive and negative attitudinal meanings, there are many other dimensions and facets of evaluation that can be associated with semantic prosody. These could include judgments of morality, social acceptability, or appropriateness, among others.

In the context of this study, we argue that, as terms become more prominent in news discourse after a significant event, they can acquire a specific emotional connotation, and gradually associate with new non-specialized language words over time. It is important to note that certain words, like 'ease' or 'fight', which may seem to have a particular sentiment when taken alone, actually serve as modifiers that alter the inherent emotional direction of the terms they collocate with, such as 'inflation' or 'debt'. Thus, these modifiers should be seen as general associations and are used to describe the economic situation, regardless of the sentiment expressed in the context. Thus, we adhere to the original notion of semantic prosody, which, applied to our analysis, means that a higher frequency of sentiment words with a particular polarity near an *event word* (i.e., the focus terms in our study) indicates that the event word has experimented a shift towards that polarity. Therefore, by studying the contexts in which the focus terms appear over time, we can identify changes in their conveyed sentiment.

8 Data analysis

This chapter presents four case studies of selected target terms during the Great Recession ('credit', 'debt', 'markets', and 'housing') according to the methodology described in section 2.3. Each analysis consists of three parts: (1) a table of longitudinal descriptive statistical results relating to sentiment scores, (2) yearly Usage Fluctuation Analysis of the term's collocates, and (3) a detailed discussion and qualitative illustration of the quantitative findings in the previous two parts.

Two datasets were used: a set of sentences for sentiment analysis and a set of collocations for Usage Fluctuation Analysis (UFA). The set of sentences includes all those cases in the corpus that include the target terms. The sentences were encoded in *csv* file where we also included some metadata, resulting in four data columns ('id', 'source_file', 'text' and 'date'). Duplicate sentences, as a result of a term occurring more than once in a sentence, were discarded. A second group of datasets was generated for the yearly collocates of each target term.

The sentences were processed with Lingmotif applying the SentiEcon plugin lexicon, which returned a dataset with sentiment-related data: Text Sentiment Score (TSS), and other text metrics (e.g., number of words, or number of sentiment items). We calculated quarterly sentiment averages and plotted the data according to the methodology described in. To facilitate the *peaks and troughs* analysis, we summarized the information in diachronic sentiment plots and yearly aggregated statistical charts. UFA of collocates are summarized in lists and time series charts. The third part is a qualitative interpretation with selected corpus examples that attempts to shed further light on the findings in the first two parts and, in addition, to trace relationships with the historical narrative profiles of the Great Recession.

8.1 Term 1: 'credit'

The term 'credit' in the Oxford English Dictionary (2019) is defined in its first sense as 'The ability of a customer to obtain goods or services before payment, based on the trust that payment will be made in the future'. As reviewed in Chapter 3, one of the main issues of the first stage of the global crisis was the frozen credit system. During the first years of the 21st century, the financial system offered ease of access to credit but after the bursting of the subprime mortgage bubble it came to a standstill. The optimism that sprang from the words in related news items at the beginning of the century was abruptly reversed and the term came to be enunciated with a more negative semantic orientation.

8.1.1 Sentiment analysis

Table 8.1 summarizes the frequency and sentiment data aggregated by year.

Table 8.1 Great Recession News Corpus yearly statistics for credit

Year	n	RF (pmw)	TSS AVG	TSS SD
2007	577	286.52	48.42	36.53
2008	1,214	569.26	39.06	35.29
2009	980	486.65	39.52	34.24
2010	942	418.07	41.69	34.53
2011	1,043	372.57	41.53	34.98
2012	948	302.52	44.67	35.30
2013	975	240.78	51.37	35.91
2014	992	234.70	51.84	35.13
2015	990	244.93	45.38	35.79
Total/AVG	8,661	324.81	44.50	35.54

Three stages can be clearly distinguished in the sentiment evolution of sentences containing 'credit' after processing the datasets and plotting the sentiment time series graphs (Figure 8.1).

Term 1: 'credit'

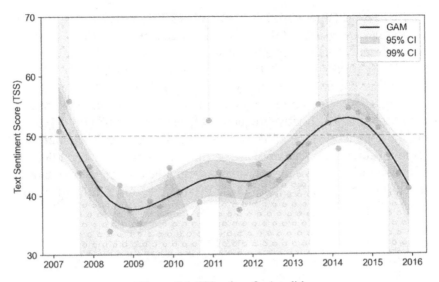

Figure 8.1 TSS values for 'credit'

The sentiment time series for this term, according to Lingmotif's TSS, suggests the existence of three distinct stages. The first one (2007) refers to the dawn of the crisis, when the word 'credit' was still used in contexts with a positive semantic orientation, reaching 55.85 in the second quarter of the year. The second phase (2008–2012) clearly corresponds with the bursting of the real estate bubble and the events that caused the freezing of the credit system, symbolized by the earthquake caused by the bankruptcy of the American global services firm Lehman Brothers on September 25, 2008. After a fall of 9 points (from TSS = 48.42 in 2007 to TSS = 39.06 in 2008), negative average values remained stable during the toughest years of the credit crisis, to finally return to a context with positive average values in 2013 (TSS = 51.84).

The last phase (2013–2015) starts with a rising TSS trend that peaks in 2014. It is important to understand that at that time the press had set in motion a type of discourse that leaned towards the reactivation of credit from central banks to private banks. By then, the US Federal Reserve was consolidating its quantitative easing program through the purchase of bank assets. Meanwhile, in the EU, the new discursive paradigm following Mario Draghi's 'Whatever it takes' statement in 2012 was underway. However, despite the recovery in average values a downward trend is apparent at the end of the sample study in 2015. Changes in diachronic TSS values are statistically significant (Kruskal- Wallis test: H (8) = 148.31; p < 0.01; One-way ANOVA: F (8, 8661) = 18.72; p < 0.001). The effect size was small (ω = 0.1227).

Figure 8.2 shows frequency data of the of the term 'credit' throughout the corpus. The relative frequency of the term in 2008 (*RF* = 485.86) nearly doubles that of 2007 (*RF* = 244.54). From this moment on, 'credit' became an event word and its mere mention became a reflection of a historical moment that affected not only the economy and financial institutions but also the daily lives of hundreds of millions of people around the world.

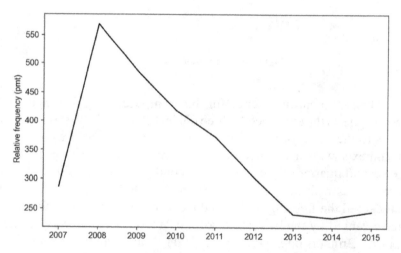

Figure 8.2 Relative frequency of 'credit' per million tokens

After this sudden boom, which is undoubtedly the result of the agitation in the news, the relative frequency decreases progressively from 2013 to the end of the study in 2015 (*RF* = 209.04). The relative frequency appears inversely proportional to the sentiment, i.e., the more 'credit' was mentioned in the news, the more negatively the context was referenced.

Term 1: 'credit'

8.1.2 Usage fluctuation analysis

Table 8.2 summarizes the results to Usage Fluctuation Analysis applied to the term, that is, the evolution of the collocations of 'credit' in the corpus. UFA provided sets of different types of collocations that can be used to identify the associations with the different grammatical categories that appear with the target term. As for the analysis of examples, we will use the three phases identified in the peaks and troughs analysis.

Table 8.2 UFA analysis of 'credit'. Negative words are in bold

CONSISTENT	*card* (2007–2015), **crunch** (2007–2015), *debit* (2007–2015), *score* (2007–2015)
INITIATING	*detail* (2015–), *experian* (2015–), *extend* (2015–), *investment-grade* (2015–), *junk* (2015–), *tax* (2015–2015), *u-turn* (2015–), *union* (2015–), *universal* (2015–), **unsecured** (2015–),
TERMINATING	**squeeze** (–2009), *subprime* (–2008), **tight** (–2009), **turmoil** (–2008)
TRANSIENT	*freeze* (2007–2009), *applicant* (2007–2010), *issuer* (2007–2011), *deserve* (2007–2015), **crisis** (2008–2009), *line* (2008–2009), *revolving* (2008–2009), *availability* (2008–2012), *triple-a* (2008–2012), **default** (2008–2013), *swap* (2008–2013), **downgrade** (2008–2015), *rating* (2008–2015), *height* (2010–2011), *check* (2010–2013), *agency* (2011–2012)

8.1.2.1 First phase (2007)

The first phase of analysis corresponds to the period immediately prior to the beginning of the crisis (year 2007). The collocates in this period are mostly neutral, such as 'credit card' (logDice = 9.83) or 'credit score' (logDice = 8.18). From the third quarter of 2007 onwards, the negative collocates began to emerge, especially 'credit crunch' (logDice = 8.97), as it became one of the main expressions used to refer to the event. This last unit started in the specialized field and ended up being vulgarized and its mention became a synonym of the ongoing crisis. Some examples are given in (1) to (6) below, all highlights in bold are ours.

> (1) Now, with the dollar down more than 40 percent against the euro and the economy hamstrung by a deep **credit crunch**, a less assured America has become increasingly reliant on foreign capital.

(2) Chancellor Alistair Darling has said he wants a return to 'old-fashioned banking' from the complex, highly-leveraged business model that has left the banks vulnerable to the **credit crunch** that began in the US.

(3) It is not surprising that in the growing **credit crunch** the market should start to become alarmed about its future viability.

(4) The result was a **credit crunch** – the secondary banks found the financial environment much more bracing, with money both hard to come by and expensive.

(5) The bank is not likely to be the only one affected by the credit crunch.

(6) A **credit crunch** is going to hit industries like private equity and hedge funds very hard indeed.

The first co-occurrence of 'credit' with 'crisis' (logDice = 5.43), still below our threshold (logDice > 7), was published in *The New York Times* in August 2007. A further 14 occurrences are found until December 2007. All these cases were related the problems of the banks to finance themselves, as illustrated by examples (7) and (8).

(7) The **crisis** in world **credit** markets has cast a shadow over the financing of a number of big deals.

(8) He also knows that the late-summer turmoil in global bond markets because of the subprime housing problems and the ensuing **credit crisis** could complicate his analysis.

8.1.2.2 Second phase (2008–2012)

During the second phase (2008–2011), the context of 'credit' is characterized by more collocations with domain-specific units and generally negative sentiment such as 'tighten' (logDice = 8.59 in 2008) or 'squeeze' (logDice = 8.75 in 2008). On the other hand, the collocation score of neutral words such as 'tax' (logDice = 5.05 in 2008) remains stable during this period.

The paradigm shift dictated by the economic situation and reflected in the sentiment of news texts during this interval is quite apparent. The word 'credit' in the press, and by extension in the streets, was invariably associated with economic crisis. This is clearly observable through the rapid rise of the collocates 'crunch' (logDice = 11.36 in 2008) and

Term 1: 'credit'

'default' (logDice = 8.51 in 2008), which now show very similar frequencies to lexically established items such as 'card' (logDice = 10.18 in 2008). As can be seen in examples (9) and (10), in 2008, 'credit crunch' was already an established collocation, commonly used with verbs in present perfect to refer to recent events.

(9) The arrival of the **credit crunch** last summer has made it extremely hard for indebted businesses to refinance while the commercial property market slowed dramatically with asset values falling.

(10) However, the **credit crunch** has meant the banks that financed the mega deal have struggled to sell on the debt, dubbed the '£800m gorilla' in the City.

However, from 2012 onwards, the collocation 'credit crunch' (logDice = 10.10 in 2012) was mainly used with the past simple tense, which implies that the situation is not ongoing, though its consequences persist at the moment of writing. Examples (11) and (12) illustrate this.

(11) Coked-up bankers caused the **credit crunch**, according to the former drug tsar David Nutt.

(12) That simply doesn't compare to the 150% bubbles we saw in some of the countries that were hit by the **credit crunch**.

The third negative sentiment word highlighted is 'default' (logDice = 9.08 in 2011), which occurs in clearly negative contexts. 'Default' refers to the failure to meet legal obligations of a loan, such as a missed mortgage payment or unpaid bond. In fact, both private and public defaults took place during this period (Lehman Brothers' in September 2008, with over $600 billion in debts, and Greece, with $138 billion in March 2012). Some examples are shown in (13) to (15) below.

(13) For a student, a **default** can destroy a **credit** record, making it hard even to rent an apartment, let alone buy a home.

(14) As the financial crisis deepened, hundreds of banks and thrifts closed and thousands more were saddled with bad loans and **credit** card **defaults**, costing the industry billions of dollars.

(15) Banks and card companies are bracing for a wave of **defaults** on **credit** card debt in early 2009, and they are vying with each other to get paid first.

In addition, 'credit default swap' is the fourth most frequently used collocation in 2010 (logDice = 9.13). This is a financial product that involves a hedging transaction where the buyer makes periodic payments to the seller and receives a payout if the security defaults. The collocation is widely associated with negative sentiment throughout the corpus and is closely linked to the banking crisis.

Credit default swaps collapsed after the bursting of the bubble of subprime mortgage in 2007. Prior to 'default' becoming a relatively common occurrence in most 'credit default swap' contracts, premium payments from the buyer to the seller were small and unregulated, making them highly speculative. The 'credit default swap' market became a cause for concern among regulators after the collapse in 2008 of the investment bank Bear Stearns. The extension of credit default swaps led to the perception that Bear Stearns was vulnerable, restricting its access to wholesale capital and eventually forcing its sale to JP Morgan. Some examples are given in (16) to (19).

(16) In addition, institutions that had bought **credit default swaps** from Bear Stearns, insurance policies that protect against corporate bond defaults, were scrambling to undo those trades as the firm's ability to pay the claims looked dicier.

(17) As the fund was being wound down, UBS said about 70 percent of its losses came from exposure to **credit default swaps**.

(18) The banks have faced public criticism since the financial crisis for the opaque manner in which their traders bought and sold **credit default swaps**, a type of financial contract that allows investors to speculate and hedge against losses and that figured prominently in the crisis.

(19) Buffett, known as the 'Sage of Omaha' once warned that **credit default swaps** were 'weapons of financial mass destruction'.

The collocate 'rating' was not present in the 2007 ranking, but it ranked first in 2008. Collocation figures remained stable (logDice > 8) until the end of the analyzed timeline.

Rating agencies are firms that rate credit products according to the debtor's ability to make payments. These agencies played a prominent role in various parts of the crisis starting with the subprime crisis from the fall of 2007. The junk mortgage packages were negligently rated by the Big Three: Standard & Poor's, Moody's, and Fitch Ratings. By the end of 2009, more than half of the AAA-rated collateralized debt obligations issued at the end of the mortgage bubble were rated as *junk*. The overt complicity between rating agencies and financial institutions was the trigger for the credit crisis, ultimately causing the collapse of the three major banks during the bubble: Lehman Brothers, Merrill Lynch, and Bear Sterns.

'Rating' is a neutral term in isolation, and as such was labeled in SentiEcon. However, the sentiment of the context in which the use of the credit-rating collocate is unequivocally negative for the period 2008–2010. Collocates such as 'insufficient', 'cannot secure', or 'junk' appear regularly in the neighborhood of the term 'credit'. A simple concordance search in the corpus reveals the close relationship of the term with the turbulent economic context, as illustrated by examples (20) to (26) below.

(20) At the moment most car firms, having insufficient **credit ratings**, cannot secure a loan worth more than £200m from the EIB fund without government guarantees.

(21) Standard & Poor's confirmed that situation after it cut its long-term **credit rating** on the company to BBB from A and said more downgrades were likely.

(22) Buffett can't qualify for the best **credit rating**.

(23) But these deals are only as good as the party on the other side, and when Security Capital's crucial **credit** rating was cut to junk this year, the potential that the company would pay out on the arrangement dimmed.

(24) Just as in the mortgage markets, a sterling **credit** rating – the bond insurer's seal of approval – is no longer trusted.

(25) Its **credit** ratings were cut yesterday, adding to fears that it could become the next victim of the financial crisis.

(26) The banks say they are worried about the **credit** ratings of the countries that have been rescuing them.

Once the first part of the crisis was overcome from 2010 onwards, rating agencies once again became relevant in the context of a crisis of 'sovereign debt', i.e., the national debt of a country. Credit rating agencies also issue ratings for state borrowers based on their ability to repay the loans. Furthermore, credit ratings reflect not only the perceived long-term risk of 'default', but also serve to study short-term political and economic developments, which becomes a pressure strategy from the financial powers to nation-states. Between 2010 and 2011 there is a shift in the semantic field of opinion objects related to 'credit rating' and 'credit rating agencies', as these move from the field of banking to the field of governmental institutions. These trends continue during the entire timeline. Concordance search samples tend to have a negative semantic orientation, as illustrated by examples (27) to (33).

> (27) Elsewhere in Europe, **credit rating** agency Moody's downgraded Spain because of concerns over its weak growth prospects and considerable deterioration in the government's financial strength.
>
> (28) The **credit rating** agency Standard & Poor's raised its sovereign debt rating for Indonesia to BB+ last month, becoming the last of the three big agencies to rate the country one peg below investment grade.
>
> (29) The Observer Global leaders race to stem panic over US **credit rating** downgrade.
>
> (30) Iceland's **credit rating** outlook downgraded as Icesave row drags on
>
> (31) UK's **credit rating** downgraded from AAA to AA1 by Moody's
>
> (32) At the time, debt-laden Fortescue had looked to sell part of its rail and port assets after **credit ratings** AGENCY Standard and Poor's said the company was the world's most vulnerable iron ore miner to lower prices.
>
> (33) On Monday, Standard & Poor's **credit** rating AGENCY downgraded RSA's debt to A- and put it on watch for further rating action within 90 days.

8.1.2.3 Third phase (2013–2015)

Key collocates of 'credit' in this time period are domain-specific terms of generally neutral sentiment. In relation to the previous interval, the novelty lies in that the ranking here also presents units with positive sentiment, as is the case of the adjective 'cheap'. The downward trend visualized between the 2014 and 2015 TSS averages (see Figure 8.1) can be justified here by the prevalence of collocates such as 'junk' (logDice = 7.86) and 'downgrade' (logDice = 7.12).

The presence of 'cheap' credit (logDice = 7.13) in the 2014 ranking was due to highly newsworthy events: the announcement of interest rate cuts by the ECB as a prequel to the Draghi Plan for quantitative easing. The interest rate cut was positively received, but it is necessary to mention that some cases highlight interpretative views and comments that question the positivity of the phenomenon. These reflect the low initial demand for lower-priced credit and the reluctance of EU central powers to such policies. Some examples found in the 2014 subcorpus are given in (34) to (39).

(34) John Leech, head of automotive at consulting group KPMG, said that while **cheap credit** had been great for driving sales, **cheap credit** is essential for driving growth in the 18-member currency zone.

(35) **cheap credit** is essential when households and businesses are close to going bust.

(36) Mario Draghi, the ECB president, is expected to tell his audience today that he is waiting to see how his previous attempts at offering cheap credit are faring before considering QE.

(37) ECB president Mario Draghi has responded to the lack of growth in the eurozone with **cheaper credit** for banks in the hope they will increase their lending to businesses and consumers.

(38) Financial markets were surprised to find limited demand for the ECB's **cheap credit** scheme.

(39) Germany wants the ECB to keep its powder dry, claiming **cheap credit** will lead to rampant inflation.

Our analysis ends with the last observation on the collocation of 'credit' with 'downgrade' (logDice = 8.05) and 'junk' (logDice = 7.86) in 2015. That year, these co-occurrences continued to be prevalent, primarily due to ongoing economic and geopolitical challenges. The Chinese economic slowdown, declining oil prices, and volatile global financial markets contributed to the 'downgrade' of credit ratings for several emerging markets, leading to a surge in the issuance of 'junk' bonds. Furthermore, the Greek and Puerto Rican debt crisis persisted, leading to further downgrades and labelling of its bonds as 'junk'. Additionally, the Federal Reserve's decision to raise interest rates resulted in concerns over the impact on the creditworthiness of various corporations and countries.

(40) And tonight, Standard & Poor's took the first step towards cutting Greece's **credit** rating further into **junk** territory.

(41) Residents began leaving for the mainland in droves, and Puerto Rico's **credit** was **downgraded** to **junk**, making borrowing extremely expensive.

8.2 Term 2: 'debt'

The term 'debt' is defined in the Collins Cobuild (2019) in its first sense as 'something that is owed, such as money, goods, or services', in its second sense as 'bad debt': 'a sum of money that has been lent but is not likely to be repaid', and in its third sense it is defined as 'an obligation to pay or perform something; liability'.

Debt is the basis of contemporary economy. Most of us have mortgages or loans and as such cannot be considered to be a concept inherently positive or negative. It serves as a necessary tool for individuals and businesses to make significant purchases or investments. Mortgages and loans enable people to acquire homes, start businesses, or pursue education. However, debt carries both positive and negative implications. It can be seen as a means of progress and wealth creation (good debt) or as a burden leading to financial distress (bad debt). The distinction lies in the purpose, management, and ability to repay the debt. Responsible financial management is essential to navigate the potential risks and benefits associated with indebtedness.

After the stall of the financial system in 2008, changes in the use of the term 'debt' were suddenly reflected in the news. The bursting of the subprime bubble was followed by generalized a lack of credit access. Consequently, individuals, private companies of all sizes and public institutions were unable to pay their lenders. As the level of indebtedness snowballed, the financial framework of the Western world cracked.

In 2009, governments bailed out private financial companies, allegedly to avoid a greater evil. The sovereign debt crisis spread throughout the European Union, mainly in the weaker economies: Portugal, Ireland, Italy, Greece, and Spain. To aggravate this, the Eurozone crisis rested on a monetary union without fiscal union, with very significant differences in social and material conditions (e.g., public pensions) between member states. The seams of the political system busted at all levels and exposed all kinds of corruption schemes and the preferential treatment of government to larger financial institutions. Thereafter, nation-states were unable to pay or refinance their public debt or to bail out highly indebted banks without the whip of the so-called Troika: the infamous triad formed by the European Commission, the European Central Bank and the International Monetary Fund.

Fifteen years later, and after another large financial crisis, we can affirm that the response capacity of European leaders was very limited and did not make great efforts to protect the population. This asymmetry of conditions turned the debt crisis into a political crisis that weakened the foundations of the European Union and caused a social emergency that permeated all layers of society, causing special damage to the weak. In fact, millions of jobs were destroyed (Spain and Greece exceeded the 27 % unemployment threshold), tens of thousands lost their homes and the echoes of cuts in health care, education, and basic social benefits can still be heard.

8.2.1 Sentiment analysis

Table 8.3 summarizes the frequency and sentiment data aggregated by year.

Table 8.3 Great Recession News Corpus yearly stats for 'debt'

Year	n	RF (pmw)	TSS AVG	TSS SD
2007	392	194.66	46.09	35.68
2008	706	331.05	42.57	36.59
2009	949	471.25	45.37	36.74
2010	1,139	505.50	41.26	35.46
2011	1,869	667.63	38.67	33.90
2012	2,270	724.39	42.51	34.13
2013	1,251	308.94	42.71	35.19
2014	1,314	310.89	43.29	35.99
2015	2,066	511.13	45.02	34.89
Total/AVG	11,956	448.39	42.68	35.14

As with the previous term, three stages can be clearly distinguished in the sentiment evolution of sentences containing 'debt' after processing the datasets and plotting the sentiment time series graphs (Figure 8.3).

The Text Sentiment Score curve shows a very long trough. Two different trends can be distinguished: a decreasing period (2007–2011) and a rising period (2012–2015). Initial quarterly averages are above the positive threshold in the first two quarters of 2007. There is a downward trend, after scores sink in 2008, until it reaches its record low in 2011. Even if from this point on TSS average does not surpass the threshold of positivity (TSS = 50), there is a clear upward trend.

Changes in diachronic TSS values are statistically significant (Kruskal-Wallis test: H (8) = 57.44; p < 0.01; One-way ANOVA: F (8, 11956) = 6.91; p < 0.001). The effect size was small (ω = 0.063).

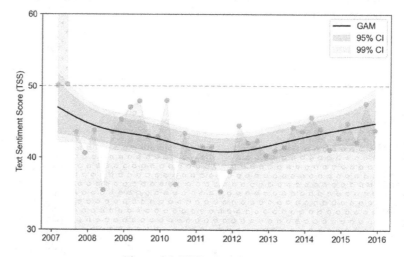

Figure 8.3 TSS values for 'debt'

The first stage corresponds to the dawn of the credit crisis in the year 2007, a second three-year stage starting with a steep decline to negative sentiment values (2008–2011) characterized by a negative sentiment score after a sudden drop and a subsequent more progressive decline until reaching the historical minimum in 2011. A final stage takes place in 2012–2015 with slightly upward trend with symmetry in the scores, similar to those of the second stage.

As for the number of occurrences of the term, Figure 8.4 plots the relative frequency of the term pr million tokens. In the first period (year

2007), the relative frequency of the term starts from a score of 46.09, with 392 occurrences in that year's subcorpus ($RF = 194.66$).

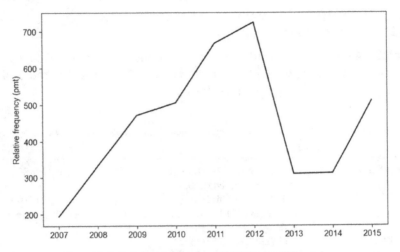

Figure 8.4 Relative frequency of 'debt' per million tokens

The second period (2008–2011) begins with a decline of 4 points in 2008 (TSS = 42.57) in which it continues to decrease until in 2011 (TSS = 38.67). There is a sharp rise in the relative frequency passing from $RF = 331.05$ in 2008 to $RF = 724.39$ in 2012. Here we find the same phenomenon as in the analysis of 'credit' as an event word: the more frequent a term is in the press discourse, the more negative the sentiment of such sentences is. This may provide evidence to Bednarek/Caple's (2012) *negativity* criterion of newsworthiness, as the press generally informs of negative events, in detriment of positive ones, generally using emotional or evaluative language in order to increase the information's newsworthiness.

The third period (2012–2015) reflects a slight upward trend in sentiment averages that consistently exceed 40%. The frequency drops by half (308.94 and 301.89 in 2013 and 2014). However, it increases again in 2015 ($RF = 511.13$) following a new episode of events related mainly to the crisis between Greece and the EU. This increase in frequency can signal a consolidation of the term as a prominent and recurring factor in the press discourse. Undoubtedly, 'debt' became an event word since 2008 and a key concept in the crisis-related discourse of that period.

8.2.2 Usage fluctuation analysis

Table 8.4 contains the results of applying Usage Fluctuation Analysis to this dataset. Again, we will use the three phases identified in the peaks and troughs analysis to structure the analysis.

Table 8.4 UFA analysis of 'credit'. Negative words are in bold, positive words are underlined

CONSISTENT	obligation (2007–2014), relief (2007–2015), repay (2008–2015), unsecured (2008–2015)
INITIATING	**crisis** (2010–), **default** (2010–), **pile** (2010–), ratio (2010–), sovereign (2010–), **mountain** (2011–), national (2011–), net (2013–)
TERMINATING	collateralized (–2011)
TRANSIENT	instrument (2008–2010), load (2008–2010), collector (2008–2012), short-term (2008–2012), refinance (2008–2013), saddle (2009–2010), collateralised (2009–2011), **burden** (2009–2014), holder (2009–2014), **distressed** (2009–2015), repayment (2009–2015), restructure (2009–2015), restructuring (2009–2015), **downgrade** (2010–2013), service (2010–2013), owe (2010–2014), coverage (2011–2012), euro (2011–2012), insure (2011–2012), mature (2011–2012), rolling (2011–2012), writedown (2011–2012), yield (2011–2012), ceiling (2011–2013), g.d.p. (2011–2013), level (2011–2013), eurozone (2011–2015), **haircut** (2011–2015), **unsustainable** (2011–2015), peripheral (2012–2013), collection (2012–2014), household (2012–2014), reduce (2012–2015), overhang (2013–2014)

8.2.2.1 First phase (2007)

The first phase of analysis corresponds to the period immediately prior to the explosion of the crisis (2007). In this phase, the use of 'debt' provides a descriptive character of the economic situation without a clear preponderance of a specific sentiment in the context. For this section of the timeline, UFA just returned the collocate 'obligation' and 'collateralized', which fit into the domain of finance and are neutral and predictable. In the examples, factual and evaluative segments alternate interchangeably. What is inferred after considering these examples is that text containing 'debt' in 2007 tended to use the term as a mere macroeconomic indicator, as illustrated by examples (42) and (43).

> (42) With variations, the same trends have persisted since 2002, when the U.S. government again began adding to the national **debt**, after a brief period of paying debt down.
>
> (43) Critics say that the sale will lead to higher prices for users to pay off $24.5 billion in new **debt** that the buyers put on TXU.

Primarily, this refers to 'collateralized debt obligations' (CDOs), which refer to a type of asset-backed security that was originally developed as an instrument for the corporate debt markets. From 2002 on, they were used as a means to refinance mortgage-backed securities. By 2007, the CDO market was dominated by subprime mortgages. Mentions in the corpus relate to their application to incentivize the flow of subprime mortgages that led to the subprime crisis of 2007–2009. In almost all occurrences, negative polarity is prevalent and words such as 'inability', 'slowed', 'loss' or 'disastrous' are found.

> (44) The biggest mistakes included Merrill's large investment in **collateralized debt obligations** and subprime lending and the company's inability to sell when the markets slowed.
>
> (45) That news came as a shock to many of the firm's executives, who were distressed that Morgan Stanley, which was not a major underwriter of **collateralized debt obligations**, would record such a large trading loss.
>
> (46) The strategy produced substantial profits for a time, but also resulted in a complex and ultimately disastrous trade in **collateralized debt obligations** earlier this year that led to the $3.7 billion write-down.
>
> (47) Sean Egan, the co-founder of Egan-Jones, an independent bond rater, believes that MBIA and the other big bond insurers will be saddled with billions of dollars in losses as **collateralized debt obligations** stuffed with subprime debt – so-called C.D.O.'s – they have insured continue to go south.

8.2.2.2 Second phase (2008–2011)

During the second phase of analysis (2008–2011), the context of 'debt' is characterized by more co-occurrences with domain-specific units as many collocates with negative sentiment emerged, such as 'default', 'burden' or 'crisis'. Most of these terms relate the main concerns of the period.

Many occurrences referenced 'unsecured' debt, a 'burden' that needed to be 'refinanced' or 'saddled' to avoid a 'downgrade'. The fear of terms related to what we can call 'bad debt' reflected fears and dangers of a possible default that would spread worldwide if no action was taken.

At the end of this period, as nation-states encountered difficulties in obtaining credit, the issue of 'sovereign debt' came to the forefront. In 2013, Greece's sovereign debt stood at 161 %, Italy's at 126 %, Portugal's at 120 %, France's at 90 %, the UK's at 89 %, and Spain's at 85 %, in comparison to a global average of 64 %.

The collocation 'burden' ranks consistently high in collocation ratios since 2009 (logDice = 8.21 in 2009, 8.34 in 2010, and 8.74 in 2011), particularly in conjunction with 'debt'. The term 'debt burden' refers to a substantial amount of money owed that presents difficulties for repayment, implying potential default. This departure from neutral depictions of 'debt' acknowledges the negative connotations and consequences associated with indebtedness. The prevalence of this collocation reflects a shift towards recognizing the subjective experiences and detrimental effects of debt in the period.

After studying the semantic prosody, the term is related to lexical units of an equally negative character, such as 'struggle', 'hampered', 'heavy', 'load', 'difficulties' or 'struggle'. Some examples from the 2008–2011 subcorpora are given in (48) to (52) below.

> (48) It denied that the decision was influenced by the spectre of BAA's £9.3bn **debt burden**, which the airport owner is struggling to finance.
>
> (49) The unusually heavy **debt burden** means Tribune's bankruptcy is not a harbinger for the newspaper industry, said Rick Edmonds, a media business analyst at the Poynter Institute.
>
> (50) 'Our country does not need just another spending bill, particularly not one that will load future generations with the **burden** of massive **debt**,' he said.

Term 2: 'debt' 111

> (51) Smaller lenders stand to lose £200m from move McCarthy & Stone, Britain's biggest retirement home builder, is facing possible administration because lenders are struggling to agree how to tackle its £900m **debt burden**.
>
> (52) The company has been struggling with its **debt burden** since June and its prospects have been hampered by the difficulties retirees are having in selling their homes in a plunging market in order to buy McCarthy & Stone properties.

Another relevant collocate in this timeline is 'default', also characterized by consistent collocation ratios (logDice = 8.06 in 2010 and 8.01 in 2011). It refers to the failure to fulfil the legal obligations or conditions of a loan, such as mortgage payments or bond repayments upon maturity. This definition inherently carries a negative connotation within its contextual usage. Notably, the period under consideration witnessed significant defaults, including the bankruptcy of Lehman Brothers in 2008, which marked a private default, and the largest sovereign default in March 2012 when Greece declared bankruptcy. The global financial crisis triggered a domino effect, leading to numerous companies and institutions facing liquidity problems as a consequence of the credit system's collapse. The semantic prosody associated with 'default' is predominantly negative, encompassing related terms such as 'precipice', 'hard', 'subordinated', 'falls' and 'risk'.

> (53) Mr. Fuld was referring to investors' panic after Russia defaulted on its **debt**, pushing a big hedge fund to the precipice.
>
> (54) There was only light trading of credit-default swaps, which allow investors to protect against the risk of a company's defaulting on its **debt**, and those trades have been a leading indicator about the health of banks.
>
> (55) Moreover, Mr. James said, about 60 percent of those companies have loans with relatively few restrictions, making it harder for these holdings to default on their **debt**.
>
> (56) Tribune's papers were down 19 percent in the third quarter – and some major newspapers have defaulted on **debt** or been put up for sale, with no takers.
>
> (57) Worldwide, there are about $55 trillion of these contracts, which enable people to make side bets on whether borrowers will default on their **debts**.
>
> (58) They either default on the **debt** or take bolder measures.
>
> (59) How can investors trust something issued by West Brom when the nationalised Bradford & Bingley is defaulting on its subordinated **debt**?

(60) After suffering sharp falls last week, world stock markets have now recovered their poise, with investors less concerned that Dubai World might default on its **debts** and spark global turmoil.

During the latter part of the study period, the 'credit crisis' turned into a 'debt crisis' (logDice = 7.74 in 2010, 9.57 in 2011 and 9.24 in 2012). This shift coincided with the emergence of the Eurozone debt crisis, which had already begun to unfold. In several member countries, private debts arising from the housing bubble transformed into sovereign debt after the private bank bailouts and the subsequent government-imposed austerity measures.

In the 2010–11 subcorpora, certain metaphors and nouns were employed to describe the Eurozone countries, particularly Greece, which was heavily affected. Metaphors such as 'under assault' and nouns like 'victim', 'pressure', 'protests', and 'cuts' were used to depict the situation. Furthermore, the discourse conveyed a sense of an uncontrollable phenomenon through verbs like 'snowballing' or 'sucked into' that emphasized the perceived lack of control and the escalating nature of the crisis in a relatively short period. The examples illustrate the intense pressure, protests, and perceived loss of control experienced during the economic turmoil.

(61) Share prices in Europe had slid on Wednesday when France was sucked into the eurozone **debt crisis**.

(62) Greece's place in the list is perhaps the most assured as its **debt crisis** continues and it comes under assault from speculators.

(63) A deal has been reached to help Greece tackle its **debt crisis**, after negotiations between Europe's leaders in Brussels this morning.

(64) Athens could announce further austerity measures to tackle its **debt crisis** next week, under intense pressure from financial markets, despite widespread protests against existing spending cuts.

(65) The multi-millionaire private equity boss at the centre of the **debt crisis** at music group EMI has spelled out the lengths to which he is going to avoid UK tax.

(66) Greece's **debt crisis** has dominated headlines since the socialists revealed the country's public deficit would reach 12.7% of GDP – nearly twice that

Term 2: 'debt' 113

>   predicted by the former conservative government – within weeks of taking office last October.
>
> (67) Sitting in the sun-dappled square where Seixal's old town meets the River Tagus, Umberto Da Silva was clear about who would suffer as Portugal became the latest victim of Europe's snowballing sovereign **debt crisis**.

The term 'debt ceiling' refers to constitutional limits on government deficits, aimed at preventing excessive spending beyond revenue and controlling the growth of public debt to ensure long-term fiscal sustainability. In 2011, the debt ceiling became a significant political crisis in both the United States and Europe.

The US Congress engaged in a debate over raising the debt ceiling, which is typically a routine approval process. However, the Republican Party demanded deficit reduction negotiations in exchange for raising the debt ceiling, risking potential default on bonds if the government failed to act. This crisis had the potential to trigger another wave of the international financial crisis. Eventually, a partial agreement was reached, just two days before the deadline. The crisis led to high market volatility and a decline in US bond ratings.

In Europe, a new reform of the Stability and Growth Pact (SGP) was proposed in March 2011, focussing on automatic sanctions for those violating deficit or GDP parameters. Germany and France, along with other EU countries, took steps towards a fiscal union within the Eurozone, implementing stringent budget rules and automatic sanctions for non-compliance. In December 2011, Eurozone members agreed to regulate parameters regarding the 'spending ceiling' and introduce automatic sanctions for violations. This agreement required Spain to undergo an express constitutional reform without a referendum, which further heightened the crisis of legitimacy in a climate of widespread protests and diminishing trust in the political class.

The sentiment of the words in the neighborhood of 'debt ceiling' found in our dataset, in both the United States and Europe, is predominantly negative. The term is frequently associated with negative elements such as 'battle', 'downgrade', 'risk', and 'miscreants'. This negative sentiment underscores the contentious nature and adverse implications associated with discussions surrounding the debt ceiling, highlighting the challenges and controversies faced by governments in managing their finances within these constraints. Examples (68) to (72) illustrate this.

(68) The Starbucks boss said he knew he had to speak out after watching Democrats and Republicans slug it out over raising the **debt ceiling**, an argument that contributed to ratings agency Standard & Poor's decision to downgrade US debt.

(69) Obama accused the Republicans of using the raising of the **debt ceiling**, which he said was normally routine, as a lever to force the Democrats to agree to deep spending cuts that would hit the poorest in society while leaving the wealthiest unscathed.

(70) There was widespread alarm in Washington this month when S&P, followed by Moody's and Fitch, other credit rating concerns, warned that the soaring federal debt and the political standoff over raising the **debt ceiling** had placed the nation's credit rating at risk.

(71) In return for the German concession, Van Rompuy was instructed to come up with proposals by the end of the year to strengthen the stability pact which sets **debt** and deficit **ceilings** for the eurozone and introduce new sanctions for fiscal miscreants.

(72) The agreement, in the wake of a nasty and protracted battle over the **debt ceiling**, was worked out as both the White House and Congress were beginning to feel pressure from voters who said they have grown tired of political fights that hurt working Americans and the economy.

As a link to the next stage, the collocates 'sovereign' and its quasi-equivalent 'national' emerge in the corpus from 2010, as news articles focus on their connection to the sovereign debt crisis that primarily affected Europe.

The eruption of the sovereign crisis, following the Greek crisis and its subsequent contagion, became a new episode of the global crisis. Analysis of examples from the 2010–2011 subcorpus reveals that the most immediate collocation for 'sovereign debt' is 'crisis'. During this period, 'crisis' transitioned from being an infrequent element in discourse, associated with macroeconomic indicators, to a key term within the domain. It is noteworthy that references to sovereign debt predominantly occur in a lexical and contextual environment characterized by negative sentiment. Sentences (73) through (80) are examples of this.

Term 2: 'debt' 115

(73) With the euro zone facing a **sovereign debt** crisis that has much further to unravel, there were already signs in August that the UK's exports to key trading partners France, Germany and the Netherlands were suffering.

(74) Tony Tyler, director general of Iata, said: "On the good news side, it appears that a worsening of Europe's **sovereign debt** crisis has been avoided for now."

(75) Banco Santander, the largest bank in Europe, moved today to assuage fears of a looming **sovereign debt** crisis in Spain after Standard and Poor's (S&P) cut the country's credit rating.

(76) Because the ratings agencies use slightly different methodologies, there is no single list of AAA-rated **sovereign debt**.

(77) Gurría's comments came as interest rates on Italian **sovereign debt** rose back above 6% and the gap between Italian and German bond yields ballooned to the widest level since the single currency was created.

(78) Quoting a document which it said was prepared by the German finance ministry, Der Spiegel said that a new Greek currency could lose as much 50% of its value if Greece pulls out of the eurozone, leading to an explosion in Greek **national debt** and crippling its banking system.

(79) Italy plans to sell off its national treasures; Greece is said to be keen to offload some surplus bits of islands ; now the right-wing Crawley-based Thomas Malthus Institute, under its president Stan Muccia, has drawn up a draconian austerity package aimed at wiping out Britain's £800bn **national debt**.

(80) In Europe, the various **national debt** crises remain unresolved, with a continued monopoly of banker-friendly austerity programs, and their predictable consequences of rising unemployment and stagnation.

8.2.2.3 Third phase (2012–2015)

The collocates identified during this final phase reflect the persistent state of economic distress in Europe, despite the emergence of certain mitigating factors. Notably, collocates such as 'crisis' (logDice = 9.24 in 2012) and 'burden' (logDice = 8.88 in 2012) maintain a stable presence throughout this period, indicating the continued challenges associated with the debt situation. However, a noteworthy development is the appearance of new collocates with positive sentiment, exemplified by words like 'relief' (from logDice = 7.54 in 2014 to 10.48 in 2015) and 'reduce' (logDice = 7.47 in 2015) respectively, suggesting a glimmer of optimism amidst the prevailing circumstances.

Greece emerges as one of the key entities in the Eurozone crisis, prominently affected by its economy's severe recession and a significant decline of 25 % during the analyzed period. The issue of bailout conditions for Greece sparked intense debates, particularly in 2015, when tensions escalated between the country and the European Union. The newly elected government's left-leaning approach and their call for the renegotiation of bailout terms led to a standoff. Ultimately, in July 2015, a referendum was held to determine economic management and the terms of a new bailout. The situation was marked by the perception that the debt burden of the European Union was unsustainable and could not be afforded.

The collocation of 'debt' with 'reduce' is consistent, signalling positive semantic prosody throughout the analyzed period. Upon examining the concordances, it becomes evident that this collocation is often used in the context of assuming an improvement in the economy, as expressed by modal verbs such as 'could' or 'should'. Furthermore, there are instances where the clause 'to reduce the debt...' is employed, as a recipe to stimulate economic growth in the face of challenging circumstances. Examples (81) through (86) illustrate this situation.

(81) Shaun Donovan, the housing secretary, has said the settlement will be a catalyst that proves that **reducing** mortgage **debt** is cost-effective for lenders.

(82) These changes could also **reduce** household **debt.**

(83) DEBTS should be '**reduced** organically through growth, or opportunistically when less distortionary sources of revenue are available,' the IMF's researchers argue.

(84) No dividends have been paid since the 2007 deal with spare cash used to **reduce** its **debt**, which at the last count stood at £7bn.

(85) To **reduce** the **debt** to 124% by 2020, the ministers were putting together a package of steps including a debt buyback funded by a eurozone rescue fund, reducing the interest rate on loans and returning eurozone central bank 'profits' back to Greece.

(86) 'This year, I think, there are three priorities: to stabilize economic growth, which is not too big of a problem,' to stabilize the prices of goods, 'where already it looks like there could be some pressure,' and to **reduce** the risk from hidden **debt**, like off-book wealth management products, said Zhao Xijun, deputy director of the Finance and Securities Institute at Renmin University in Beijing.

The noun 'relief' emerges as a prominent UFA collocate, particularly in 2014 and 2015. It is used to describe a set of measures aimed at alleviating the economic burden caused by the debt crisis, primarily in the case of Greece. During this interval, 'relief' is portrayed as something demanded by those affected by the crisis, rather than offered by the economic powers. This is evident through the use of verbal phrases associated with confrontation ('pressing for', 'asking for', or 'pushing for') where the agents ('cash-poor Ukraine', 'left politicians', etc.) are often portrayed in opposition to the major power, especially the International Monetary Fund.

Within the context of the Euro crisis, all parties involved (the Troika, the Greek government, and economic agents) agreed on one thing: the Greek debt was unsustainable for the entire European bloc and required some form of relief measures ('measures', 'agreement', 'concessions') to be obtained through negotiation. Despite the majority of the Greek people rejecting further intervention in the Greek bailout referendum in the Summer of 2015, an agreement was reached between Tsipras' government and the Troika for a third bailout. One would expect the semantic prosody to be positive in sentiment in such a case. However, the examples in the corpus reveal co-occurrences with neutral or negative terms, as exemplified by sentences (87) to (93).

(87) The International Monetary Fund has said it will refuse to take part in the bailout unless there is an 'explicit and concrete' agreement on **debt relief** for Greece.

(88) But eurozone governments have so far resisted substantial **debt relief** and are implacably opposed to any measure that could write off some Greek debts, otherwise known as a 'haircut'.

(89) Politicians instructed by the radical left prime minister to fight Athens's corner, in what is being billed as the very last chance to cut a deal after five months of fruitless talks, will press for **debt relief** in exchange for concessions demanded by international creditors.

(90) It is asking for **debt relief** under the terms of the November 2012 bailout agreement, and it wants to be able to take steps to deal with the humanitarian crisis caused by the 25% collapse in the size of the economy over the past five years.

(91) After the power change, the cash-poor Ukraine started pushing for **debt relief**.

(92) Even excluding **debt relief**, however, financial assistance to the least-developed countries fell in 2014, the OECD said.

(93) As chairman of the International Institute of Finance – an industry group that represents the interests of large investment banks like Deutsche, Goldman Sachs and Morgan Stanley – he played a primary role in negotiating an agreement that provided crucial **debt relief** for Greece.

8.3 Term 3: 'markets'

During the Great Recession, 'markets' became one of the prominent event words in the news. World leaders undertook political actions, primarily aimed at justifying economic measures, that had significant impact on citizens and their rights, such as labor law reforms and public policy cuts. These reforms were frequently justified as a demand from 'markets', which in this sense, and used in plural refers is an abstract, collective noun that, rather euphemistically, made reference to a conglomerate of transnational financial corporations. Decision makers emphasized the need to appease these markets in order to implement extensive economic measures. In retrospect, nevertheless, these actions were revealed to be staunch defences of corporate interests that mostly salvaged failed private actors with public money.

Undoubtedly, this discourse was widely reproduced by news outlets. The term 'markets' quickly became an event word, with its usage doubling between 2007 and 2008. Relevant collocates of this term in this period are the words 'calm' (logDice = 6.72 in 2008 or 7.75 in 2010) and 'reassure' (logDice = 7.01), which our linguistic intuition would consider more typical of specific domains such as psychology or childcare rather than the language of economics and finance, as illustrated by examples (94) to (97).

(94) The US Federal Reserve and European Central Bank tried to **calm** the money **markets** by promising to provide liquidity during the expected credit market freeze.

(95) Economists were split on the merits of the move, with some calling it a mistake but others suggesting it would bring **calm** to the **markets**.

Term 3: 'markets' 119

(96) Other banks, he said, gambled incorrectly that **calm** would return to the **markets** after investors returned from summer vacations.

(97) Business leaders hope that the rescue package will thaw out the frozen credit **markets** and restore **confidence** in struggling banks.

It is also worth mentioning that we find many cases of a particular metaphorical usage that connects the world of finance and with mythological (Greek or Aztec) narratives: markets-gods, invisible and capricious were mediated by the politicians-priests, and demanded sacrifices in the form of 'capital injections' ('providing liquidity', 'rescue packages') or 'austerity measures' to restore confidence.

(98) If not, then clearly the **market gods** sanctified New Labour's economic credentials.

(99) If it does, it is hardly the first time IBM or any other big company will have sacrificed its workers to appease the **gods of Wall Street**.

(100) So, it would be a real sign of progress if there was evidence that the **gods of the financial markets** were re-learning the virtue of patience, thus setting an example to mortals.

(101) It's the feeling that if we make a sacrifice that somehow the **gods** would be appeased.

(102) The **Gods** That Failed: How Blind Faith in **Markets** Has Cost Us Our Future

8.3.1 Sentiment analysis

Table 8.5 summarizes the frequency and sentiment data aggregated by year.

Table 8.5 Great Recession News Corpus yearly stats for 'markets'

Year	n	RF (pmw)	TSS AVG	TSS StDev
2007	628	311.85	56.09	36.48
2008	1,259	590.36	46.12	36.80
2009	761	377.90	53.55	36.98
2010	1,081	479.76	51.97	36.67

Continued

Table 8.5 Continued

Year	n	RF (pmw)	TSS AVG	TSS StDev
2011	1,845	659.06	48.92	36.12
2012	2,015	643.02	52.54	36.04
2013	1,851	457.12	57.06	35.18
2014	2,166	512.47	54.66	35.92
2015	2,762	683.32	46.83	36.64
Total/AVG	14,368	538.85	51.48	36.41

The TSS data series in Figure 8.5 shows two peaks and two troughs. Three different trends can be distinguished: two declining (2007–2009, 2014–2015) and one rising (2010–2013). Initial quarterly averages are above the positive threshold in 2007, 2009–10 and 2012–14. Changes in diachronic TSS values are statistically significant (Kruskal-Wallis test: $H(8) = 159.46$; $p < 0.01$; One-way ANOVA: $F(8, 14368) = 19.68$; $p < 0.001$). The effect size was small ($\omega = 0.101$).

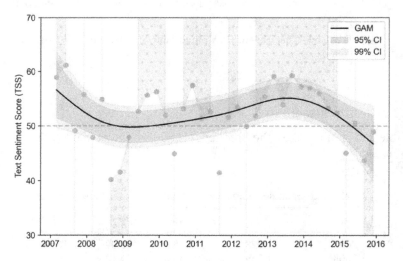

Figure 8.5 TSS values for 'markets'

Term 3: 'markets' 121

According to these results, we can identify three phases: (a) 2007, (b) 2008–2011, (c) 2012–2014 (d) 2015.

The first stage corresponds to the period before the bursting of the subprime bubble. Quarterly averages between 2008 and 2011 follow a W-shaped pattern with a record negative low in the third quarter of 2008 and a positive high in the fourth quarter of 2009. This fluctuation may reflect the uncertainty caused by the crisis as the average sentiment score of sentences including the word 'markets' dropped to TSS = 40. Scores remain positive during most quarters since the 2012–2014 interval. Finally, in 2015, TSS scores return negative values (TSS = 29.77), except for the slight increase in sentiment in the second quarter (TSS = 50.53) but declines again in following quarter (TSS = 43.72) and remains negative overall. Among other factors, it is important to note that the worsening of the euro political crisis turned out to be one of the main factors behind the decline in sentiment scores.

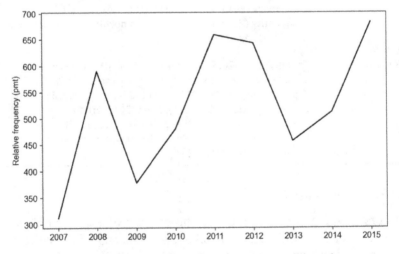

Figure 8.6 Relative frequency for 'markets' per million tokens

In terms of relative frequencies, the word 'markets' is much more frequent than the other three study terms. Nonetheless, as with the other terms, an increase in relative frequency goes along with a sound change in sentiment. For example, the use of 'markets' nearly doubled between

2007 and 2008 (RF = 311.85 and 590.36, respectively) while in the same interval the sentiment score dropped from 56.09 to 46.12. A plateau is apparent in the 2011–2012 interval, and then a new peak in frequency occurs in 2015 (RF = 683.32), also coinciding with the decline in TSS averages (46.83).

8.3.2 Usage fluctuation analysis

Table 8.6 contains the results of applying Usage Fluctuation Analysis to this dataset. As for the analysis of examples, we will use the four phases identified in the peaks and troughs analysis.

Table 8.6 UFA analysis of 'markets'. Negative words are in bold, positive words are underlined

CONSISTENT	emerging (2007–2015), **turmoil** (2007–2015),
INITIATING	currency (2013–), exchange (2014–), foreign (2013–), authority (2014-), cma (2014-), competition (2014–), frontier (2014-), **rig** (2014–)
TERMINATING	-
TRANSIENT	**tight** (2008–2009), **plunge** (2008–2010), wholesale (2008–2012), overseas (2008–2014), capital (2008–2015), commodity (2008–2015), rbc (2008–2015), **volatile** (2008–2015), **panic** (2009–2011), bond (2010–2015), <u>fast-growing</u> (2011–2014), cmc (2011–2015), stock (2011–2015), equity (2011–2015), sharply (2011–2015), **volatility** (2011–2015), international (2012–2015)

8.3.2.1 First phase (2007)

Discursively, the effects of the bursting of the real estate bubble were noticed after the third quarter of 2007. An analysis of the collocates of 'markets' in this year reveals an abundance of words that belong to the domain of economy (e.g., 'emerge', logDice = 8.07), which is recognized as a verb by the SketchEngine's lemmatizer, but which in most cases refers to the adjective 'emerging' in the phrase 'emerging markets'. The term refers to high-growth countries that have the characteristics of a developed market, but do not meet the standards. This includes, for example, the BRIC (Brazil, Russia, India and China)

Term 3: 'markets' 123

countries, which may be considered, in fact, developing markets. No particular sentiment trend stands out in the concordances. Some examples are shown in (103) to (107).

(103) We are one of the few global power companies that not only is operating in developed countries but also in emerging markets, which, with respect to electricity, have much higher growth rates.

(104) Toyota prides itself on pampering customers, but analysts are reporting weak or uneven service at Toyota sales subsidiaries, particularly in emerging markets like China and India.

(105) Brought in from PepsiCo last year to turn Kraft around, Ms. Rosenfeld faced weak sales in emerging markets, few innovative products and a portfolio of brands that are about as fresh as a 'Brady Bunch' rerun.

(106) Cellphone operators in emerging markets, and particularly in India, are adding customers at breakneck speed, making them attractive acquisitions for more sluggish Western companies.

(107) But it could well become a cautionary tale, whether for investors in emerging markets or for Venezuela – which, Skye says, may be liable for up to $6 billion if all the bondholders press their claims.

From July 2007 onwards, 'turmoil' (logDice = 7.42) emerged as a collocate and continued throughout the year. This is probably due to the uncertainty in the markets after the bursting of the real state bubble. In the neighborhood of this collocation, we find more negative elements related to the shock and the expansion of the crisis ('unremitting', 'uproar', 'creep in', 'rocked' or 'problems'). From this moment on, 'markets' becomes an event word, as they become not only an important actor but also a kind of abstract indicator, as the state of markets served as a proxy measure of the crisis.

(108) On Tuesday, after a month of almost **unremitting turmoil** in financial markets.

(109) The reason was the **turmoil** in the mortgage markets and the resulting gyrations in share values on the stock exchanges.

(110) But a cautiousness has begun to **creep in**, brought on by recent turmoil in the markets, **uproar** over a lavish birthday party for the private equity executive.

(111) sly bailey, the chief executive, said **turmoil** in the financial markets was a key factor.

(112) Mr. Schott said that the scrutiny, which was first reported yesterday in tax analysts, a prominent trade publication, was not related to the recent **turmoil** in the mortgage markets.

(113) No financial institution has escaped damage from the turmoil that **rocked** the credit markets in July and August as **problems** in the subprime mortgage market widened.

8.3.2.2 Second phase (2008–2011)

During the second stage the average market sentiment scores are grouped into three sub-phases: (a) a fall to negative values in 2008 corresponding to the bursting of the credit bubble, (b) a rise to positive values in 2009, partially motivated by momentary recovery due to the US government intervention, and (c) a relapse after the debt crisis between 2010 and 2011. The sentiment averages clearly respond to historical events and the separation of the two crises can be clearly seen here. While 2008 saw the explosion of the credit crisis and the subsequent intervention of the US government, 2010 saw the movements that mark the beginning of the Eurozone crisis. In this year, Greece is rescued for the first time and a multilevel crisis begins in the European Union.

It should be noted here that while in 2008 and in the 2010–2011 period there are collocates with negative sentiment (e.g., 'turmoil', 'volatile', 'crisis'), in 2009 there are only four collocates with logDice > 7, two of which are negative ('panic' and 'tight').

The first collocate to be studied is 'financial', with consistent log-Dice scores (7.97 in 2008, 7.26 in 2010, and 8.31in 2011) throughout the study interval. As can be seen in the examples drawn from the corpus, there are many references to events of the economic crisis, e.g., the collapse of Lehman Brothers. Therefore, negative-sentiment words, such as 'unsettled', 'unstable' or 'pandemonium', regularly appear in the vicinity of the term, as exemplified by sentences (114) to (119).

(114) And Mr. Matolcsy, an economist who once served as Hungary's representative at the European Bank for reconstruction and development in London, is not known for his diplomacy, and has sometimes **unsettled financial markets**.

(115) The announcement left the **financial markets** convinced that it would be September at the earliest before the key us interest rate was raised from its current range of 0–0.25%.

Term 3: 'markets'

(116) Why can't countries borrow from the **financial markets**?

(117) The 81% taxpayer-owned bank is reported to be among at least six major players in the **financial markets**, including deutsche bank in Germany and Citigroup in the us, caught up in the cartel investigation.

(118) Claims that Barclays illegally took advantage of the **pandemonium** in **financial markets** in 2008 in order to acquire the US operations of bust investment bank Lehman Brothers at an unfair price have been thrown out by a New York bankruptcy court.

(119) A showdown between the most powerful leaders in the eurozone and George Papandreou is under way amid increasing **concern** about the Greek prime minister's plan to hold a referendum and the impact it is having on **financial markets**.

Another recurring collocate throughout the interval 2008–2010 is the adjective 'volatile'. Markets are said to be volatile when the stock market rises and falls by more than 1 % over a given period. In the economic domain, volatility is an indicator, and as such has a potentially negative sentiment because, in most cases, the higher the volatility, the higher the risk. 'Volatile' acquires significance in the list of collocations in the years 2008 (logDice = 7.6) and 2010 (logDice = 8.07), coinciding with a time of great instability in the markets, especially in the flow of credit. The study of the semantic prosody of the adjective during this interval allows us to identify other highly negative lexical units near 'volatile', as well as units specific to ongoing events ('housing', 'recession'). During these years, to talk about markets was to talk about lack of stability and volatility. Especially in this interval, any news regarding the development of events in the economy translated into falls in the stock market. We find many examples of such negative words: 'irrational', 'beast', 'slack', 'poor', 'depressed', 'crisis', 'yo-yoing', 'damage', 'risky', among others, as illustrated by examples (120) to (131).

(120) These firms have been curtailed slightly by recent regulations aimed at making the **markets** less **volatile**.

(121) **Markets** are extremely **volatile** and **irrational** – all of a sudden people are dealing with a different **beast**,' Cass said.

(122) The Petrobras sale is also expected to attract interest from energy investors, who have rushed into natural resource companies as they perceive them to be safer than the recently **volatile** credit and equity **markets**.

(123) The dollar's descent accelerated, particularly against the euro, in the second half of 2007 as falling housing prices, **volatile** equity **markets** and **slack** consumer spending pointed to a possible recession in the United States.

(124) The hedge fund community is battling against **poor** returns, given **volatile** credit and equity **markets**, and against forthcoming tougher regulation.

(125) While oil markets look well supported by Opec, BP expects gas **markets** to remain **volatile** and refining margins to remain **depressed** for the foreseeable future.

(126) The stream of junk bond sales seen earlier this year, which included the £500m bond issue by Manchester United, has slowed to a trickle over the past few weeks because of **volatile markets** and the Greek debt **crisis**.

(127) Stock **markets** were described as **volatile** with many shares **yo-yoing** throughout the day as traders attempted to assess the **damage** from the decline in creditworthiness of Spain and Greece.

(128) Financial experts have predicted that there could be more blockbuster sales to come as ultra-wealthy individuals look for alternative ways to invest their money away from the **risky**, **volatile** financial **markets**.

(129) The two sides are arguing about whether this reflected a shift in **volatile markets**, impairing the value of assets held on Lehman's floor, or whether it was quietly inserted into transaction documents.

(130) Fund managers are seeking these situations as **volatile** equity and credit **markets** have made it more **difficult** to gain returns from tracking indexes, such as the FTSE 100.

(131) The hedge fund community is **battling** against **poor** returns, given **volatile** credit and equity **markets**, and against forthcoming tougher regulation.

8.3.2.3 Third phase (2012–2014)

During the third stage of analysis (2012–2014), the mean of the sentiment scores for 'markets' are always positive, corresponding with a valley in the relative frequency of use of the term in the corpus.

In this interval, 'markets' usually appears in the discourse in relation to the opening of new horizons of international expansion after almost five years of credit stagnation. Compared to the previous phase there is a lesser number of references to the economic and institutional crisis financed by many national markets.

Term 3: 'markets' 127

References to growth are evidenced by the only emergent collocate we find, 'fast-growing' (logDice = 7.35 in 2012). Obviously, growth is a desirable economic factor, and it is labeled as such is recorded in the SentiEcon plugin lexicon. The sentences in this period have a general positive sentiment that responds to a better situation for multinational companies from Europe and the United States that, despite the crisis in their countries of origin, had sought to expand in emergent markets, which were not so hit by the crisis; therefore, multiple references to Asia or Africa are found. Generally speaking, sentences in which 'fast-growing' and 'market' co-occur tend to present positive semantic prosody and tend to include specialized lexical units of a positive nature, such as 'bigger dividends', 'profitable' or 'spur'. Examples (132) to (135) illustrate this.

(132) EADS chief Tom Enders confirms push into **fast-growing** Asian **markets** It would be a 'mistake' to ignore Asia-Pacific, which will account for a third of new aircraft deliveries by 2032, says EADS boss EADS chief executive Tom Enders also said the company's €34bn merger with BAE Systems was not being driven by cost savings.

(133) HSBC warns on jobs as cost-cutting continues In a strategy update, bank shifts focus to **fast-growing markets** and considers bigger dividend payouts to shareholders HSBC is focusing on cost-cutting and **fast-growing markets**.

(134) Tesco, which has agreed a memorandum of understanding with CRE, said on Friday morning that the proposed tie-up was consistent with its 'strategy of focusing on profitable routes to growth in **fast-growing** but less mature **markets**, with a disciplined approach to the allocation of capital'.

(135) The government has been keen to build links with China as part of its efforts to get British companies trading with **fast-growing** emerging **markets**.

8.3.2.4 Fourth phase (2015)

The final stage of analysis corresponds to the year 2015, in which the mean sentiment scores of sentences including 'markets' descend to the threshold of negativity to an average of TSS = 46.83, while their frequency balloons in just one year to RF = 683.32. As was the case in the second interval, 'markets' again becomes an event word that is put in relation to lexical units reflecting the turbulence of that year's on-going affairs. Two UFA collocates with negative sentiment are representative of the events that occurred that year: 'rig' and 'turmoil'.

'Rig' refers to a series of fraudulent actions related to two cases of free market manipulation: that of the LIBOR, an interest rate average calculated from estimates submitted by the leading UK banks, and the artificial adjustment of currency exchange rates. Six years after the collapse of the financial system and the billion-dollar bailout of banks with public funds, it was shown that the major banking powers broke the laws of free competition and systematically manipulated interest rates to benefit from operations, or to give a false solvency impression.

In May 2015, US and British arbitration authorities fined six of the world's largest banks $6.357 billion for violating antitrust laws. Among the effects on the public, the manipulation of interest rates made subprime mortgage payments more expensive than they should be, as interest rates were artificially altered every month to inflate banking benefits.

These events are reflected in the prosody of 'markets'. Despite the increased use of the term in the corpus the negativity is not diluted and the collocation of the study term with 'rigged' acquires great significance (logDice = 8.66). Besides 'rigging', other negative words such as 'fined', 'penalties' or 'accusations' stand out as collocates. In 2015, talking about markets is clearly related to manipulation and lack of free competition. Examples (136) though (141) illustrate this.

(136) It was among six major banks hit with £2.6bn of penalties in November for **rigging** the foreign exchange **markets**, where £3.5tn changes hands each day.

(137) It has already been fined for **rigging** interest rate and currency **markets** and faces nearly £2bn of penalties for the way it sold mortgage bonds in the runup to the 2008 banking crisis.

(138) It also comes after a year when the industry has faced big fines for **rigging** financial **markets**.

(139) He was docked £500,000 for control failures at the bank, including accusations of **rigging** the foreign exchange **markets**.

Term 3: 'markets' 129

(140) RBS is braced for scrutiny of its pay deals following last year's £400m fine for **rigging** foreign exchange **markets** and because of outstanding payments that were promised to chief executive Stephen Hester when he left in 2013.

(141) The payouts come as the bank awaits a fine for its role in **rigging** foreign exchange **markets** for which it has set aside £1.25bn and amid reports that the banks is poised to settle a civil case in the US, alongside Citi, for £550m.

Finally, 'turmoil' becomes a more significant collocate (from log-Dice = 6.55 in 2014 to 8.06 in 2015). The shift in the semantic orientation of the context of 'markets' during 2015, as well as the increase in its frequency is related to several international events: (a) the economic turbulence following the election of Alexis Tsipras in Greece, (b) the end of the Euro-Swiss franc parity, (c) a large number of mergers and acquisitions between multinationals, and (d) the stock market crash in the Shanghai exchange. In the neighborhood of the collocation, multiple negative elements are present, such as 'casualties', 'surge', 'plunging' or 'collapse'.

(142) The People's Bank of China's last rate cut in August triggered **turmoil** in world **markets** after Beijing combined the decision with a 2% reduction in the yuan's value.

(143) West Ham FC sponsor Alpari UK has become one of the biggest casualties of Thursday's **turmoil** on currency **markets** sparked by the Swiss central bank abandoning its attempt to peg the franc against the euro.

(144) Economists warn the pickup in UK exports could prove short-lived given a strong pound and the recent **turmoil** in global **markets** sparked by China's shares rout.

(145) Janet Yellen, the Fed's chair, made clear that its recent decision to delay a long-planned increase in rates was a result of the **turmoil** in emerging **markets**, in particular China.

(146) The SNB's announcement on 15 January that it had scrapped its cap of SFr1.20 to the euro – the centrepiece of its monetary policy since September 2011 – unleashed a surge in the value of the currency and **turmoil** on the foreign exchange **markets**.

8.4 Term 4: 'housing'

The study of 'housing' in the context of the Great Recession is interesting because of its deep-seated connection to the very foundations of the crisis that emerged in the early 2000s. During this period, major Western economies experienced exceptionally low mortgage interest rates and relaxed consumer loan requirements, fostering an environment where individuals, companies, and governments had easy access to substantial loans. Banks actively encouraged real estate-linked investments, driven by the false assumption that housing prices would never decline. This created an economic bubble that was rapidly reflected in discourse and debates surrounding the economy. By analyzing the intricacies of the key term 'housing' in context, we aim to obtain valuable insights into the formation and subsequent effects of the crisis via the lexicon, as well as the discursive underpinnings between housing markets, financial institutions, and economic stability.

Behind the booming market was a complex financial mechanism that began to show signs of weakness. The thriving market hid a complex financial mechanism that began to show signs of weakness. Borrowers bought overpriced homes and thousands of people were unable to make their mortgage payments. Compounding the problem, monthly payments increased due to adjustable-rate mortgages. By 2006, home prices stopped rising at breakneck speed and in some cases began to stagnate or even decline. Shortly thereafter, the subprime crisis exploded in 2007. Banking weakness after the credit freeze, coupled with a discourse of shock and fear caused bank failures. The public saw high-level institutions fail, and the discourse of panic increased. In a historic event, it was demonstrated that real estate market funds beyond being infallible led to the breakdown of the economy.

8.4.1 Sentiment analysis

Table 8.7 summarizes the frequency and sentiment data aggregated by year.

Term 4: 'housing'

Table 8.7 Great Recession News Corpus yearly stats for 'housing'

Year	n	RF (pmw)	TSS AVG	TSS SD
2007	290	144.01	47.90	36.07
2008	459	215.23	35.24	34.45
2009	252	125.14	41.46	37.24
2010	300	133.14	39.45	33.34
2011	351	125.38	47.16	37.01
2012	330	105.31	44.98	34.70
2013	594	146.69	54.43	37.45
2014	732	173.19	56.28	35.15
2015	671	166.01	54.07	36.68
Total/AVG	3,979	149.23	48.64	36.57

The visualization of the data Figure 8.7 reveals the presence of one trough and one peak. Overall, the TSS data series depicts a decreasing trend from 2007 to 2012, followed by a rising trend from 2013 to 2015. This indicates a shift from relatively positive sentiment to more negative sentiment and then a subsequent recovery towards more positive sentiment in the timeline.

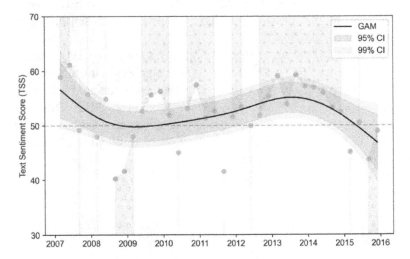

Figure 8.7 TSS values for 'housing'

We identify two phases: (a) 2007–2011, corresponding to the full stage of the housing bubble and its consequences, and (b) 2012–2015. While in the first stage the sentiment score is very negative for most of the timeline, the second stage is positive in its entirety.

From 2013 to 2015, there is a rising trend in the TSS average. In 2013, the TSS average rises 10 points and reaches its highest point at 54.43, indicating a more positive sentiment. This upward trend continues in 2014 with a TSS average of 56.28 and in 2015 with a TSS average of 54.07. Despite the TSS average not surpassing the positivity threshold (TSS=50) from 2011 onwards, there is a noticeable upward trend in sentiment during this period.

Changes in diachronic TSS values are statistically significant (Kruskal-Wallis test: $H(8) = 57.44$; $p<0.01$; One-way ANOVA: $F(8, 3979) = 5.21$; $p < 0.001$). The effect size was small ($\omega = 0.092$).

From 2007 to 2012, there is a decreasing trend in the TSS average. In 2007, the TSS average is 47.90. However, it starts to decline in 2008 to 35.24, indicating a shift towards more negative sentiment. This downward trend continues in 2009 with a TSS average of 41.46, and in 2010 with a TSS average of 39.45. By 2011, the TSS average slightly recoups to 47.16, but still remains negative. In 2012, the TSS average increases to 44.98, indicating a slight improvement in sentiment compared to the previous year.

Regarding the frequencies, as Figure 8.8 shows, in 2008 the maximum frequency ($RF = 215.23$ in 2008) coincides with the minimum score in sentiment. Thereafter, the frequency of 'housing' in the corpus drops to its historical minimum ($RF = 105.31$) in 2012. This is followed by an upward trend in frequency until reaching the peak in 2014 ($RF = 173.19$) and starting again a downward trend with a drop at the end of the timeline in 2015 ($RF = 166.01$).

Term 4: 'housing'   133

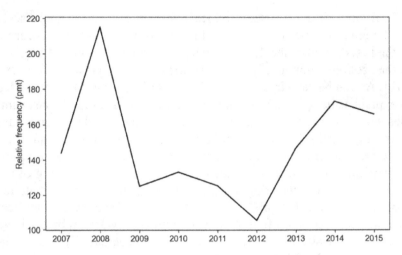

Figure 8.8 Relative frequency of 'housing' per million tokens

8.4.2 Usage fluctuation analysis

Table 8.8 displays the evolution of the collocations of 'housing' resulting from UFA. As for the analysis of examples, we will use the two phases identified in the peaks and troughs analysis.

Table 8.8 UFA analysis of 'housing'. Negative words are in bold, positive words are underlined

CONSISTENT	affordable (2007–2015), boom (2007–2015), **bubble** (2008–2015)
INITIATING	cool (2014-), ladder (2014-), **shortage** (2013-),
TERMINATING	**slump** (-2008)
TRANSIENT	**bust** (2008–2012), **burst** (2011–2013)

8.4.2.1 First phase (2007–2012)

Unlike in the previous analyses, the timeline of the study begins in the middle of the real estate crisis and starts with negative values that will be maintained during the years of the credit crisis. This broad presence of negative UFA collocates justifies the low levels of the annual average sentiment scores.

'Bubble' is a consistent collocate for the economic discourse of the timeline. Its use here refers to the real estate bubble that occurred in the first decade of the 2000s. The term, which is considered negative in the economic domain, is one of the top collocates between 2007 and 2011. As can be seen in examples (147) to (152), the term is often used to explain as being at the root of the current crisis. Moreover, the examples show that, for years, financial analysts failed to detect and warn of the incipient crisis, as the bubble prices and the profits and interest earned on credit and debt were highly profitable for them, ignoring critical voices warning of the consequences of the bursting of the bubble. It is also interesting to note that both newspapers attribute the responsibility of this bubble to several actors in a somewhat uncritical way: among others, we find the financial blocks ('German banks') and professionals ('swaps', 'investors') as well as the actual victims, the citizens ('young Greeks, Irish and Spaniards'), who are accused of entering into a cycle of 'borrowing binges' when trying to access a basic good such as a home.

(147) German banks helped to finance **housing bubbles** in the periphery – usually not directly, but through loans to other banks.

(148) Mr. Greenspan brushed aside worries about a potential **bubble**, arguing that **housing** prices had never endured a nationwide decline and that a bust was highly unlikely.

(149) By contrast, the younger Greeks, Irish and Spaniards went on borrowing binges, driven in particular by rising demands for new homes and consumer goods that, in several cases, turned into **housing bubbles** before going bust.

(150) The Sage of Omaha has glibly defended ratings agencies, declaring that they 'made the same mistake as 300 million other Americans' in failing to spot a **housing bubble** and a global financial crisis.

(151) In the United States, during the **housing bubble**, the mythology was that we could build an economy out of endless debt, and no harm would come because the foundation upon which that debt was built – the price of housing – was indestructible.

(152) The swaps enabled some investors to multiply their mortgage bets, while letting others wager that the **housing bubble** would pop.

The collocate 'boom' in economy generally has a positive connotation and would be the positive counterpart of the same phenomenon described with negative sentiment by 'bubble'. It is persistently present among top collocates between 2007 and 2012 (e.g., logDice = 8.75 in 2008). Despite being positive, however, there is an important difference in the semantic prosody of this term: when 'boom' is used, lexical units with markedly negative sentiment ('collapse', 'danger', 'loses', 'devastating') tend to appear in its neighborhood, as illustrated by examples (153) to (158) below.

> (153) Banks packaged thousands of home loans into bonds known as mortgage-backed securities during the **housing boom** and sold them to investors around the world.
>
> (154) Much of the attention in the recent **collapse** of the **housing boom** has focused on those in **danger** of losing their home or facing higher monthly payments on their adjustable mortgages.
>
> (155) Legal wrangling over Wall Street's behavior during the **housing boom** has targeted virtually every step in the process, from making loans to borrowers with tarnished credit to the sale of securities engineered with the sub-prime loans.
>
> (156) At Wells Fargo, which was a major subprime mortgage lender during the **housing boom**, regulators estimated that losses on first mortgages would hit almost 12 percent of its loan portfolio if the adverse situation proved correct.
>
> (157) 'The financial shock that erupted in August 2007, as the US sub-prime mortgage market was derailed by the reversal of the **housing boom**, has spread quickly and unpredictably to inflict extensive damage on markets and institutions at the heart of the financial system,' it said.
>
> (158) Spain, which has suffered a **devastating housing boom** and bust, is also lagging behind, according to the consultancy, which says it could be a decade before either country gets its debts back to the 'pre-bubble trend'.

After the real estate 'boom' and its subsequent 'bubble', came the 'bust', one of the most significant collocates in 2008 and 2009 (logDice = 7.79, and 8.24, respectively). The bursting of the housing bubble was a global phenomenon that affected financial markets around the world ('Estonian', 'United States', 'California', 'Spain', in the examples) and it is always referred to as current events with present tense verbs. Examples (159) through (165) evidence that during a considerable time interval the effects of the bursting of the bubble were not known with certainty, as reflected by the presence of words related to uncertainty, always with a negative prosody. Among the words with which 'housing bust' co-occurs we find 'distress', 'havoc', 'casualties' or 'loss-making'.

(159) As experts debate whether we are headed for a **housing bust**, you would think that we should at least be able to define it.

(160) The Estonian response to economic **distress** contrasts sharply to the United States, where Washington is borrowing freely and desperately trying to prevent the **housing bust** from wreaking **havoc** across the economy.

(161) SunTrust Banks of Atlanta and Regions Financial of Alabama have been hard hit by the **housing bust** that has affected much of the Southeast, and their problems with commercial real estate and corporate loans have severely worsened.

(162) Like California, some other states with outsize problems from the **housing bust** are spending the money for something other than homeowner relief.

(163) Then came the **housing bust**, which demonstrated that when lenders allowed people to buy houses they ultimately could not afford, it hurt the parties – while putting the economy itself in a tailspin.

(164) Spain's central bank estimates some €180bn of potentially **loss-making** toxic real estate assets left over from the 2008 **housing bust** are held by banks.

(165) A seven-member investor group including affiliates of the billionaire George Soros and of Michael Dell, the founder of Dell, have agreed to purchase IndyMac Bank, a failed lender and one of the largest **casualties** of the U.S. **housing bust**, for $13.9 billion.

8.4.2.2 Second phase (2013–2015)

TSS values become positive during this phase, which is due to a lower frequency of negative items (such as 'bubble' or 'crash') but above all to the increase of positive lexical items such as 'cool' (logDice = 8.58 in 2014) or 'affordable' (which leads the ranking with logDice = 8.81 in 2015). However, a closer look at the examples in the corpus shows that there are many nuances in the journalistic discourse that may not be fully captured by the lexical sentiment analysis. In fact, there are many sentences that criticize the governments and banks-sponsored real estate sector's pursuit of growth that took place at this time.

'Bubble' remained the most significant collocate during 2013 and 2014 (logDice = 9.65 in 2013, and 9.21, respectively), until this was replaced by 'affordability'/'affordable' in 2015. After a mild economic recovery in the US, the economic policies implemented by Washington helped to improve the housing market. However, as appalling events were recent, fears of a new housing bubble were rekindled. This can be evidenced by negative collocates such as 'fear' or 'concerned'. Examples (166) to (171) illustrate this:

(166) Record number of estate agents raises fears of unsustainable **housing bubble** ONS data shows 562,000 people work in real estate sector – the largest number since records began in 1978 'We're no longer a nation of shopkeepers, we're becoming a nation of estate agents,' said one economist.

(167) Britain now has a record number of estate agents, official figures have revealed, underlining fears that the fledgling economic recovery is based on inflating an unsustainable **housing bubble**.

(168) MPs are also concerned that the monetary policy committee, which sets interest rates, will be forced to clamp down on a **housing bubble** by raising rates prematurely.

(169) Land Registry Official data showing house prices have increased 3.4% in a year on average reignites fears of **housing bubble**.

(170) Carney, the central bank governor, to wonder if there might be a **housing bubble** in the making and if so, what should be done about it.

(171) Hoping to deflate a potential **housing bubble**, the Bank of England recently put a cap on lenders, saying that no more than 15 percent of their loan portfolios can consist of mortgages in which borrowers are lent amounts that exceed 4.5 times their income.

In contrast to the previous stage, here they use the present tense to discuss an emerging housing 'boom' (logDice = 8.01 in 2013 and 7.25 in 2015). While 'boom' has positive connotations in general, here we find it used in contexts both with a positive ('surge', 'taken off') and negative ('jeopardise', 'warning') prosody. The corpus shows that the press did not receive with much positivity the improvements of the economic results in a sector that in less than five years had blown up the world economy. In the examples we find references to corruption ('black money') or a new wave of poor management by the banking sector ('exacerbate').

(172) The **housing boom** 'created a huge reserve of black money, especially in coastal areas', demonstrated by the 'massive use' of €500 notes, which the report claims account for 70% of all the cash in circulation.

(173) Bank of England warns **housing** market **boom** may turn to crash.

(174) **Housing boom** shifts focus to Scotland Price growth in the Scottish market is significantly outpacing London, while the average sale figure for a UK home has reached £273,000, official figures show.

(175) **Housing** market Buy-to-let **boom** could jeopardise financial stability, says Bank of England Looser lending requirements for landlords could bolster house prices but also exacerbate falls if borrowers need to sell when interest rates rise, Bank says.

(176) Since the Reserve Bank (RBA) began cutting interest rates in November 2011, the **housing boom** has taken off.

(177) In the **housing boom** that followed, a massive surge of investors entered the market, raising their share to 52%.

Finally, the logDice score of 'affordable', one of the CONSISTENT collocates, peaks in 2015 and becomes the highest ranked collocate of that year (logDice = 8.81). Examples (178) to (182) discuss critically the outcomes of the housing crisis. The management of the housing crisis left an aftermath of thousands of evictions and homeless families around the world, while the construction standstill prevented access to housing for just as many. The demand for affordable housing by the population is critically reflected in the corpus. While co-occurrences with positive sentiment words are found (e.g., 'welcomed', 'commitment'), most of the examples are negative.

(178) The Local Initiatives Support Corporation, already working with Morgan Stanley on **affordable housing**, welcomed their new commitment to funding such projects.

(179) We urgently need to build more **affordable housing** in London, but unless all new homes are made available for Londoners to buy, they won't help solve the crisis.

(180) We wanted to increase the amount of **affordable housing** for students and create a sustainable, non-exploitative, community-led housing co-operative as an alternative to the private rental market.

Term 4: 'housing' 139

(181) A Conservative victory spelled an end to Labour's pledges to introduce a mansion tax on homes worth £2m or more, and to cap rent increases in the private sector to make **housing** more **affordable** for tenants.

(182) The ratio of homes classified as **affordable housing** is 15%.

Finally, to illustrate particular problems, example sentences (183) to (186) denounce British construction companies trying at all costs to find legal loopholes to avoid fulfilling their legal responsibility to build social housing ('opacity', 'show their sums', 'to be exposed').

(183) Real estate Councils to expose developers' murky viability claims to increase cheap homes London's Islington council to publish developers' own assessments and demand evidence for profit claims to raise portion of **affordable housing** in new schemes Plans for the Mount Pleasant sorting office in Farringdon.

(184) Secretive calculations used by property developers to avoid paying for **affordable housing** are to be exposed in a bid to increase the supply of cheap homes.

(185) The opacity of developers' claims about how much profit they need to make if a scheme is to be viable, and therefore how much social housing they can afford to build, has been identified as a key reason for the fall in construction of **affordable housing**.

(186) The Guardian view on **affordable housing**: the developers must be made to show their sums.

9 Discussion and conclusions

This chapter aims to summarize the main findings described in Chapter 8 and, in addition, will reflect on the theoretical implications of these findings. This volume has been motivated by two primary research questions. First, we have aimed to explore whether the semantic orientation or connotations of terms undergo changes when the polarity of the words they co-occur with changes. Secondly, we have sought to investigate whether major historical events, particularly economic crises, have a significant impact on driving rapid shifts in the semantic orientation of terms. By addressing these questions, we have aimed to gain a deeper understanding of the dynamics of language and the influence of major historical and societal contexts.

We have studied how the language used in news articles is affected by external events in a systematic manner. Our analysis and the results we obtained offer a comprehensive view of how language can rapidly change within a short period of time in relation to a specific economic indicator during a major economic crisis. Our methodology, which involves identifying changes in sentiment and word associations, avoids making broad assumptions or drawing larger conclusions about language use in general. Instead, it focuses on the evolution of sentiment, semantic prosody, and collocations.

Several conclusions stand out from the results of our research:

1. Methodologically, our approach appears to successfully identify shifts in the semantic orientation of key terms in specialized domains. The sentiment scores provided by lexicon-based sentiment analysis tools facilitate the observation of significant shifts in the sentiment underlying the discourse. The frequency information of aggregated time series data supports

sentiment data, while Usage Fluctuation Analysis provides a solid method to triangulate data.
2. During historical events, terms become event words, and significant changes in usage occur: the collocates of the terms change, and new lexical units with a distinct semantic orientation come into play. There is a notable increase in the frequency of terms relating to the most significant events of the crisis and, in general, their collocates tend to be less specialized than they were before they became event words.
3. The combined analysis using these methods and the interpretation of results vis-à-vis the actual historical events that they describe enables us to conclude that the semantic orientation of terms in the economic-financial domain is highly susceptible to change.

An event is defined by how it is portrayed in the discourse of the press, which plays a crucial role in shaping public opinion by providing a sense of objectivity and authenticity to the reported facts. In other words, an event becomes significant when it is recognized and treated as such by the press, which establishes minimum standards for the perception of an event by the public. Our data analysis, both quantitative and qualitative, of news text published during the Great Recession offers a panoramic view of the significance and impact of how the crisis impacted the use of a set of key terms in specialized discourse. We consider that short-term sentiment changes in their usage spread when such terms become event-words, as they are 'imbued' (in Louw's terms) with the positive/negative outcome of the events of the crisis when they are described in the news. In the context of economic journalism, the discourse is mediated, involving interactions between journalists and other experts, such as politicians and economists, and the general public. This circulation of information, which allows an ordinary fact to evolve into an event, adds a lasting social significance by means of the association of a particular term with a set of collocates and, by extension, the connotations they convey over a specific timeframe. When the public reads repetitively these event words in the news, they also may acquire new connotations via the emerging word associations.

Term frequencies (Figure 9.1) evidence that the 2008 financial crisis had a profound impact on coverage, resulting in a substantial increase in the use of related terms, and this increase in usage was

Discussion and conclusions

frequently accompanied by a significant shift in their semantic orientation. Figure 9.2 shows that, in the case of 'debt' 'credit' and 'markets', there was a shift from a positive average sentiment observed before the crisis (in 2007) to a decline that reached a negative level.

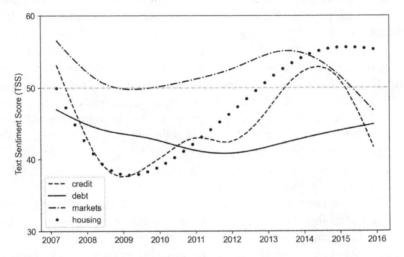

Figure 9.1 TSS trends for all study cases

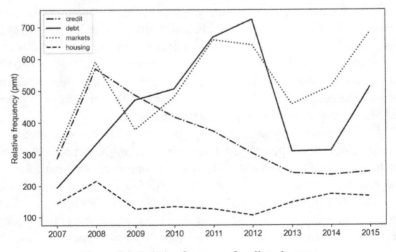

Figure 9.2 Relative frequency for all study cases

The analysis reveals that changes in the semantic prosody of these event words can be identified by Usage Fluctuation Analysis and sentiment scores. Three distinct periods were identified: pre-crisis in 2007, the crisis from 2008 to around 2012, and the European debt crisis from 2012–13 to 2015. UFA sheds light on the phenomenon by showing how the collocates of the focus terms change, from being mostly neutral and domain-specific to being mostly sentiment-laden during times of crisis. To illustrate this, 'debt' remains negative throughout the timeline while the sentiment trends of the other study terms rise to positive levels after 2012. This seems to be linked to the narrative of improvements in macroeconomic conditions in some northern Eurozone countries, coupled with the discursive shift brought about by the implementation of policies that provided some economic relief. In particular, a paradigm of this moment is the announcement of the European Central Bank's quantitative easing policies, famously encapsulated in Mario Draghi's 'Whatever it takes' speech.

From the corpus-based study, it is found that semantic prosody is a property of the lexicon that is not static, but varies over time, and these changes may be accelerated by real-world events and how these events are portrayed in the press. In accordance with Bublitz (1996), UFA allowed us to observe how words that co-occur with key terms (event words) change over a time interval and, importantly, quantitative changes in sentiment scores take place concurrently. As an example, from 2008 onwards, the frequency of 'card', a collocate of the term 'credit' that makes up a well-established multi-word unit ('credit card') was lower than several negative-sentiment, crisis-related collocates (e.g., 'crunch', 'default'). This is in agreement with Steward (2010), who considers that this type of phenomenon is an immediate 'contagion' of the pragmatic or attitudinal meaning of the term from a sudden and violent event, such as the economic crisis.

By studying language in use, specifically key terms from the economic-financial specialized domain as used in the press, it is apparent that the evaluative use of terms is present at all linguistic levels, and that this evaluative use of words in specialized language is not an exception. Thus, this finding aligns with Alba-Juez/Thompson's (2014) position, whereby the expression of sentiment about the entities being discussed is recurrent, as discussed in Chapter 4. Also, within the

Discussion and conclusions

economic/financial news domain, this feature appears to serve the purpose of influencing the audience in a manner that reflects the community of speakers' values.

Furthermore, examining economic terms *in vivo* from a sentiment perspective provides a deeper understanding of their real meaning, including the evolution their semantic prosody, and reveals the complex and flexible communicative possibilities associated with these terms. Additionally, our findings challenge the notion of terminological synchronicity, as they illustrate the evolving sentiment of terms even within short time spans, thus adding further evidence to the existing body of research that criticizes this notion, such as that by Temmerman (2000) and the collective work on diachrony by Banks (2010).

In conclusion, the proposed methodological framework effectively achieves the overall objective of this book, which is to identify trends and fluctuations in term sentiment and to establish connections with real-world events to detect changes in linguistic and sociological patterns. The comprehensive analysis of quantitative and qualitative data from a large corpus of text provides robust evidence that major social and economic events, such as the Great Recession, plays a role in shaping the evolution of a term's sentiment. The notable variations in term usage and the emergence of new collocations during a period characterized by economic challenges clearly indicate the presence of an evaluative dimension in the communicative use of economic and financial terms.

List of Figures

Figure 4.1. Du Bois's stance triangle 39
Figure 8.1   TSS values for 'credit' 95
Figure 8.2   Relative frequency of 'credit' per million tokens 96
Figure 8.3   TSS values for 'debt' 106
Figure 8.4   Relative frequency of 'debt' per million tokens 107
Figure 8.5   TSS values for 'markets' 120
Figure 8.6   Relative frequency for 'markets' per million tokens . 121
Figure 8.7   TSS values for 'housing' 131
Figure 8.8   Relative frequency of 'housing' per million tokens ... 133
Figure 9.1   TSS trends (Linear GAM) for all study cases 143
Figure 9.2   Relative frequency for all study cases 143

List of Tables

Table 1.1　Number of sentences extracted for each focus term 17
Table 1.2　Lingmotif's evaluation metrics for three-way sentiment classification 23
Table 4.1　Affect and evidentiality categories (Biber/Finegan 1989) 47
Table 8.1　Great Recession News Corpus yearly statistics for credit 94
Table 8.2　UFA analysis of 'credit' 97
Table 8.3　Great Recession News Corpus yearly stats for 'debt' .. 105
Table 8.4　UFA analysis of credit 108
Table 8.5　Great Recession News Corpus yearly stats for 'markets' 119
Table 8.6　UFA analysis of 'markets'. 122
Table 8.7　Great Recession News Corpus yearly stats for 'housing' 131
Table 8.8　UFA analysis of 'housing'. 133

References

Ahmad, Khurshid/Cheng, David/Almas, Yousif. 2006. Multi-Lingual Sentiment Analysis of Financial News Streams. *PoS*, 001.

Alba-Juez, Laura/Thompson, Geoff. 2014. The Many Faces and Phases of Evaluation. In Laura Alba-Juez /Geoff Thompson (eds.). *Evaluation in Context*. Amsterdam / Philadelphia: John Benjamins Publishing Company, 3–24.

Alessi, Glen Michael/Partington, Alan. 2020. *Modern Diachronic Corpus-Assisted Language Studies: Methodologies for Tracking Language Change over Recent Time*. Fidenza: Mattioli 1885.

Alim, H. Samy. 2011. What If We Occupied Language? *The New York Times*. Available at https://archive.nytimes.com/opinionator.blogs.nytimes.com/2011/12/21/what-if-we-occupied-language/ [Accessed on June 24, 2023].

Arrese, Ángel/Vara-Miguel, Alfonso. 2016. A Comparative Study of Metaphors in Press Reporting of the Euro Crisis. *Discourse & Society* 27/2, 133–55.

Aue, Anthony/Gamon, Michael. 2005. Customizing Sentiment Classifiers to New Domains: A Case Study. In *Proceedings of Recent Advances in Natural Language Processing (RANLP)*. Citeseer, 2–1.

Baccianella, Stefano/Esuli, Andrea/Sebastiani, Fabrizio. 2010. SentiWordNet 3.0: An Enhanced Lexical Resource for Sentiment Analysis and Opinion Mining. In *Proceedings of the Seventh International Conference on Language Resources and Evaluation (LREC'10)*. La Valletta: European Language Resources Association (ELRA), 2200–2204.

Balasubramaniam, Niroshan. 2009. User Generated Content. In Florian Michahelles (ed.). *Proceedings of Business Aspects of the Internet of Things*. Zurich: ETH, 28–34. Available at https://web.archive.org/web/20120905130300/http://www.im.ethz.ch/education/FS09/iotsem09_proceedings.pdf.

Banks, David, ed. 2010. *Aspects diachroniques du texte de spécialité*. Paris: l'Harmattan.

Batra, Siddharth/Rao, Deepak. 2010. Entity Based Sentiment Analysis on Twitter. *Science* 9/4, 1–12.

Bednarek, Monika. 2006. *Evaluation in Media Discourse: Analysis of a Newspaper Corpus*. London: Continuum.

Bednarek, Monika. 2008a. *Emotion Talk Across Corpora*. New York: Palgrave Macmillan.

Bednarek, Monika. 2008b. Semantic Preference and Semantic Prosody Re-Examined. *Corpus Linguistics and Linguistic Theory* 4/2. Available at https://www.degruyter.com/document/doi/10.1515/CLLT.2008.006/html [Accessed on February 28, 2023].

Bednarek, Monika/Caple, Helen. 2012. 46 *News Discourse*. London: A&C Black.

Benamara, Farah et al. 2012. How Do Negation and Modality Impact on Opinions? In Association for Computational Linguistics, 10–18. Available at http://dl.acm.org/citation.cfm?id=2392701.2392703 [Accessed on May 28, 2018].

Benamara, Farah/Taboada, Maite/Mathieu, Yannick. 2017. Evaluative Language beyond Bags of Words: Linguistic Insights and Computational Applications. *Computational Linguistics* 43/1, 201–264.

Biber, Douglas/Finegan, Edward. 1988. Adverbial Stance Types in English. *Discourse Processes* 11, 1–34.

Biber, Douglas/Finegan, Edward. 1989. Styles of Stance in English: Lexical and Grammatical Marking of Evidentiality and Affect. *Text-interdisciplinary Journal for the Study of Discourse* 9/1, 93–124.

Blood, Deborah J/Phillips, Peter CB. 1995. Recession Headline News, Consumer Sentiment, the State of the Economy and Presidential Popularity: A Time Series Analysis 1989–1993. *International Journal of Public Opinion Research* 7/1, 2–22.

Bloomfield, Leonard. 1933. *Language*. New York: Henry Holt.

Boiy, Erik/Moens, Marie-Francine. 2009. A Machine Learning Approach to Sentiment Analysis in Multilingual Web Texts. *Information Retrieval* 12/5, 526–58.

Bollen, Johan/Mao, Huina/Zeng, Xiaojun. 2011. Twitter Mood Predicts the Stock Market. *Journal of Computational Science* 2/1, 1–8.

Bréal, Michel. 1897. *Essai de Sémantique*. Paris: Hachette. Available at https://archive.org/details/essaidesmantiq00bruoft/page/n11.

Brezina, Vaclav. 2018. *Statistics in Corpus Linguistics: A Practical Guide*. Cambridge; New York, NY: Cambridge University Press.

Brooke, Julian/Tofiloski, Milan/Taboada, Maite. 2009. Cross-Linguistic Sentiment Analysis: From English to Spanish. In *Proceedings of RANLP 2009, Recent Advances in Natural Language Processing*. Borovets, Bulgaria, 50–54. Available at https://aclanthology.org/R09-1010.pdf.

Brown, Gregory W./Cliff, Michael T. 2004. Investor Sentiment and the Near-Term Stock Market. *Journal of Empirical Finance* 11/1, 1–27.

Brown, Tom B et al. 2020. Language Models Are Few-Shot Learners. *arXiv preprint arXiv:2005.14165*.

Bublitz, Wolfram. 1996. Semantic Prosody and Cohesive Company: Somewhat Predictable. *Leuvense Bijdragen: Tijdschrift voor Germaanse Filologie* 85/1–2, 1–32.

Bublitz, Wolfram. 2003. Emotive Prosody: How Attitudinal Frames Help Construct Context. In *Anglistentag 2002, Bayreuth – Proceedings*. Trier: Wissenschaftlicher Verlag Trier.

Buhler, Karl. 1934. *Speachtheorie. Die Darstellungsfunktion Der Sprache*. Jena: Fisher.

Cadilhac, Anaïs/Benamara, Farah/Aussenac-Gilles, Nathalie. 2010. Ontolexical Resources for Feature-Based Opinion Mining: A Case-Study. In *Proceedings of the 6th Workshop on Ontologies and Lexical Resources*, 77–86.

Cavallin, Karin. 2012. Exploring Semantic Change with Lexical Sets. In *Proceedings of the XV EURALEX International Congress*, 1018–22.

Chafe, Wallace. 1986. Evidentiality in English Conversation and Academic Writing. In Wallace Chafe /Johanna Nichols (eds.). *Evidentiality: The Linguistic Coding of Epistemology*. Norwood: Ablex, 261–72.

Chan, Samuel W. K./Chong, Mickey W. C. 2017. Sentiment Analysis in Financial Texts. *Decision Support Systems* 94, 53–64.

Chan, Wesley S. 2001. Stock Price Reaction to News and No-News: Drift and Reversal After Headlines. *SSRN Electronic Journal*. Available at http://www.ssrn.com/abstract=262452.

Chaudhuri, Arjun. 2006. *Emotion and Reason in Consumer Behavior*. Amsterdam: Routledge.

Cheung, Christy MK/Thadani, Dimple R. 2012. The Impact of Electronic Word-of-Mouth Communication: A Literature Analysis and Integrative Model. *Decision Support Systems* 54/1, 461–70.

Collins Cobuild. 2019. Debt definition and meaning. Available at https://www.collinsdictionary.com/es/diccionario/ingles/debt [Accessed on February 9, 2019].

comScore. 2012. Most Read Online Newspapers in the World: Mail Online, *New York Times* and *The Guardian*. Available at https://www.comscore.com/Insights/Infographics/Most-Read-Online-Newspapers-in-the-World-Mail-Online-New-York-Times-and-The-Guardian [Accessed on January 30, 2020].

Conrad, Susan/Biber, Douglas. 2000. Adverbial Marking of Stance in Speech and Writing. In Susan Hunston /Geoff Thompson (eds.). *Evaluation in Text: Authorial Stance and the Construction of Discourse*. Oxford: Oxford University Press, 56–73.

Cook, Paul/Stevenson, Suzanne. 2010. Automatically Identifying Changes in the Semantic Orientation of Words. In Nicoletta Calzolari (Conference Chair) et al. (eds.). *Proceedings of the Seventh International Conference on Language Resources and Evaluation (LREC'10)*. Valletta, Malta: European Language Resources Association (ELRA), 19–21.

Crowley, Terry/Bowern, Claire. 2010. *An Introduction to Historical Linguistics*. Oxford: Oxford University Press.

Dave, Kushal/Lawrence, Steve/Pennock, David M. 2003. Mining the Peanut Gallery: Opinion Extraction and Semantic Classification of Product Reviews. In *Proceedings of the 12th International Conference on World Wide Web*. Budapest, Hungary: ACM, 519–28. Available at http://www2003.org/cdrom/papers/refereed/p451/package/p451-dave.html [Accessed on March 14, 2010].

Davis, Aeron. 2011. News of the Financial Sector: Reporting on the City or to It? *Open Democracy* 31.

Deng, Dong/Jing, Liping/Yu, Jian/NG, Kwok Po. 2018. Topic-Adaptive Sentiment Lexicon Construction. 2018 First Asian Conference on Affective Computing and Intelligent Interaction (ACII Asia), 1–6. https://doi.org/10.1109/ACIIAsia.2018.8470357

Devitt, Ann/Ahmad, Khurshid. 2007a. A Lexicon for Polarity: Affective Content in Financial News Text. In *Proceedings of the Conference on Language for Special Purposes*.

Devitt, Ann/Ahmad, Khurshid. 2007b. Sentiment Polarity Identification in Financial News: A Cohesion-Based Approach. In *ACL.*, 1–8.

Devlin, Jacob/Chang, Ming-Wei/Lee, Kenton/Toutanova, Kristina. 2019. BERT: Pre-Training of Deep Bidirectional Transformers for Language Understanding. In *Proceedings of the 2019 Conference of the North American Chapter of the Association for Computational Linguistics: Human Language Technologies, Volume 1 (Long and Short Papers)*. Minneapolis, MN: Association for Computational Linguistics, 4171–86.

Dewey, John. 1939. Theory of Valuation. *International Encyclopedia of Unified Science.*

Dörnyei, Zoltán. 2007. *Research Methods in Applied Linguistics: Quantitative, Qualitative, and Mixed Methodologies.* Oxford: Oxford University Press.

Dovring, Karin. 1954. Quantitative Semantics in 18th Century Sweden. *Public Opinion Quarterly* 18/4, 389–94. Available at https://us.sagepub.com/sites/default/files/upm-assets/23161_book_item_23161.pdf

Du Bois, John W. 2007. The Stance Triangle. In Englebretson, Robert (ed.). *Stancetaking in Discourse. Subjectivity, Evaluation, Interaction.* Amsterdam/Philadelphia: John Bejamins Publishing Co., 139–82.

Ederington, Louis H/Lee, Jae Ha. 1993. How Markets Process Information: News Releases and Volatility. *The Journal of Finance* 48/4, 1161–91.

Engelberg, Joseph. 2008. Costly Information Processing: Evidence from Earnings Announcements. *SSRN Electronic Journal.* Available at http://www.ssrn.com/abstract=1107998 [Accessed on June 26, 2023].

Engle, Robert F/Ng, Victor K. 1993. Measuring and Testing the Impact of News on Volatility. *The Journal of Finance* 48/5, 1749–78.

Fairclough, Norman. 2015. *Language and Power.* Third edition. London; New York: Routledge, Taylor & Francis Group.

Fama, Eugene F. 1970. Efficient Capital Markets: A Review of Theory and Empirical Work. *The journal of Finance* 25/2, 383–417.

Farzindar, Atefeh/Inkpen, Diana. 2015. Natural Language Processing for Social Media. *Synthesis Lectures on Human Language Technologies* 8/2, 1–166.

Fernández-Cruz, Javier. 2017. Can Sentiment in Our Words Be Quantified? An Introduction to Lingmotif, a Sentiment Analysis Software Tool and Its Educational Application. *International Congress on the Didactics of the English Language* 2/1. Available at http://revistas.pucese.edu.ec/ICDEL/article/view/137 [Accessed on June 14, 2017].

Fernández-Cruz, Javier/Baixauli-Pérez, Cristóbal. 2018. Análisis de Sentimiento Con Lingmotif: Aproximación Metodológica al Análisis de Intervenciones En Series Temporales de La Valencia. In *La Simulación En Ingeniería*. Esmeraldas: PUCESE, 43–51.

Fernández-Cruz, Javier/Moreno-Ortiz, Antonio. 2020. Building the Great Recession News Corpus (GRNC): A Contemporary Diachronic Corpus of Economy News in English. *Research in Corpus Linguistics* 8/2, 28–45.

Finch, Julia/Clark, Andrew/Teather, David. 2009. Twenty-Five People at the Heart of the Meltdown ... *The Guardian*. Available at https://www.theguardian.com/business/2009/jan/26/road-ruin-recession-individuals-economy [Accessed on April 27, 2023].

Firth, J. R. 1957. A Synopsis of Linguistic Theory, 1930–1955. In *Studies in Linguistic Analysis. Special Volume, Philological Society*, 1–32.

Francis, Gill. 1986. *Anaphoric Nouns*. Birmingham: English Language Research.

Freitas, Larissa/Vieira, Renata. 2013. Comparing Portuguese Opinion Lexicons in Feature-Based Sentiment Analysis. *International Journal of Computational Linguistics and Applications* 4, 147–58.

Gablasova, Dana/Brezina, Vaclav/McEnery, Tony. 2017. Collocations in Corpus-Based Language Learning Research: Identifying, Comparing, and Interpreting the Evidence. *Language Learning* 67/S1, 155–79.

Gabrielatos, Costas/McEnery, Tony/Diggle, Peter J/Baker, Paul. 2012. The Peaks and Troughs of Corpus-Based Contextual Analysis. *International Journal of Corpus Linguistics* 17/2, 151–75.

Gallardo Paúls, Beatriz. 2017. Pseudopolítica en la red: indicadores discursivos de desideologización en Twitter. *Pragmalingüística* /25, 189–210.

Garcia, Diego. 2013. Sentiment during Recessions. *The Journal of Finance* 68/3, 1267–1300.

Garea, Fernando. 2008. La crisis deja solo al Gobierno. *El País*. Available at https://elpais.com/diario/2008/06/13/espana/121330 8006_850215.html [Accessed on April 27, 2023].

Garofalo, Giovanni. 2017. Persiguiendo Con Imparcialidad 'El Total Desprecio a La Constitución': El Léxico Valorativo En La Querella Del Fiscal de Cataluña Contra Carme Forcadell i Lluís. *Quaderns de Filologia – Estudis Lingüístics* 22/22, 79–103.

Geeraerts, Dirk. 1997. *Diachronic Prototype Semantics: A Contribution to Historical Lexicology*. Oxford, UK: OUP.

Gillmor, Dan. 2011. Occupy Language: The Struggle over Meaning. *The Guardian*. Available at https://www.theguardian.com/commentisfree/cifamerica/2011/nov/22/occupy-language-struggle-over-meaning [Accessed on June 24, 2023].

Godbole, Namrata/Srinivasaiah, Manja/Skiena, Steven. 2007. Large-Scale Sentiment Analysis for News and Blogs. *Proceedings of International Conference on Weblogs and Social Media (ICWSM)* 7/21, 219–22.

Gouws, Stephan/Metzler, Donald/Cai, Congxing/Hovy, Eduard. 2011. Contextual Bearing on Linguistic Variation in Social Media. In *Proceedings of the Workshop on Language in Social Media (LSM 2011)*, 20–29.

Goźdź-Roszkowski, Stanislaw/Hunston, Susan. 2016. Corpora and beyond–Investigating Evaluation in Discourse: Introduction to the Special Issue on Corpus Approaches to Evaluation. *Corpora* 11/2, 131–41.

Haas, Michael/Versley, Yannick. 2015. Subsentential Sentiment on a Shoestring: A Crosslingual Analysis of Compositional Classification. In *Proceedings of the 2015 Conference of the North American Chapter of the Association for Computational Linguistics: Human Language Technologies*, 694–704.

Haase, Fee-Alexandra. 2010. The Linguistic Representation of Financial Crisis. The New York Times Online, 2008–2009. *Entelequia: revista interdisciplinar* 11, 93–106.

Halliday, M. a. K. et al. 2014. *An Introduction to Functional Grammar*. Routledge. Available at https://www.taylorfrancis.com/books/9780203783771

Hamilton, William L/Leskovec, Jure/Jurafsky, Dan. 2016. Cultural Shift or Linguistic Drift? Comparing Two Computational Measures of Semantic Change. In *Proceedings of the Conference on Empirical*

Methods in Natural Language Processing. Conference on Empirical Methods in Natural Language Processing. NIH Public Access, 2116.

Hampp, T./Lang, A. 2005. Semantic Search in Websphere Information Integrator Omnifind Edition: The Case for Semantic Search. *IBM Developer Works.*

Hatzivassiloglou, Vasileios/McKeown, Kathleen R. 1997. Predicting the Semantic Orientation of Adjectives. In *Proceedings of the 35th Annual Meeting of the Association for Computational Linguistics and 8th Conference of the European Chapter of the Association for Computational Linguistics.* Association for Computational Linguistics, 174–81.

Henríquez-Miranda, Carlos/Guzmán-Luna, Jaime. 2016. Las ontologías para la detección automática de aspectos en el análisis de sentimientos. *Prospectiva* 14/2, 90–98.

Hoey, Michael. 2000. Persuasive Rhetoric in Linguistics: A Stylistic Study of Some Features of the Language in Chomskyan Grammar. In Susan Hunston/Geoff Thompson (eds.). *Evaluation in Text: Authorial Stance and the Construction of Discourse.* Oxford: Oxford University Press, 28–37.

Hoey, Michael. 2005. *Lexical Priming.* London: Routledge.

Holborow, Marnie. 2015. *Language and Neoliberalism.* Routledge.

Hu, Minqing/Liu, Bing. 2004. Mining and Summarizing Customer Reviews. In *Proceedings of the Tenth ACM SIGKDD International Conference on Knowledge Discovery and Data Mining.* Seattle: ACM, 168–77. Available at http://portal.acm.org/citation.cfm?id=1014073&dl=GUIDE&coll=GUIDE&CFID=80308782&CFTOKEN=73139236

Hunston, Susan. 2011. *Corpus Approaches to Evaluation: Phraseology and Evaluative Language.* New York: Routledge. Available at http://public.eblib.com/EBLPublic/PublicView.do?ptiID=592987

Hutto, Clayton J./Gilbert, Eric. 2014. VADER: A Parsimonious Rule-Based Model for Sentiment Analysis of Social Media Text. In *Proceedings of the International AAAI Conference on Web and Social Media,* 216–25.

Israel, Michael. 2011. *The Grammar of Polarity: Pragmatics, Sensitivity, and the Logic of Scales.* Cambridge: Cambridge University Press.

Available at https://www.cambridge.org/core/books/grammar-of-polarity/E8CC889E319D4F2B4B1692CBDF3E3DBD

Janot, Pascale. 2012. Histoire d'une Crise, Histoire d'un Terme : De Quelques Stratégies Discursives Autour Du Terme Subprime Dans La Presse Généraliste Française. In Laurent Gautier (ed.). *Les Discoures de La Bourse et de La Finance*. Forum Für Fachsprachen-Forschung, Berlín: Frank und Timme, 47–62.

Jiménez Gómez, Isidro. 2015. Los 7 'mejores' eufemismos económicos de la Troika. *El salmón contracorriente*. Available at http://www.elsalmoncontracorriente.es/?Los-7-mejores-eufemismos-642 [Accessed on May 1, 2023].

Jullian, Paula M. 2009. An Exploration of Strategies to Convey Evaluation in the 'NoteBook' Texts. PhD Thesis. University of Birmingham.

Kamp, Hans/Reyle, Uwe. 1993. *From Discourse to Logic*. Dordrecht: Kluwer.

Kamps, Jaap et al. 2004. Using WordNet to Measure Semantic Orientations of Adjectives. In *LREC*. Citeseer, 1115–18.

Kant, Immanuel. 1785. *Groundwork for the Metaphysics of Morals (Trad. A. Wood, 2002)*. New Haven: Yale University Press.

Kennedy, Alistair/Inkpen, Diana. 2006. Sentiment Classification of Movie Reviews Using Contextual Valence Shifters. *Computational Intelligence* 22/2, 110–25.

Kilgarriff, Adam et al. 2014. The Sketch Engine: Ten Years On. *Lexicography*, 7–36.

Kim, Soo-Min/Hovy, Eduard. 2004. Determining the Sentiment of Opinions. In *Proceedings of the 20th International Conference on Computational Linguistics*. COLING '04, Stroudsburg: Association for Computational Linguistics. Available at https://doi.org/10.3115/1220355.1220555 [Accessed on March 8, 2019].

Klein, Frederick C/Prestbo, John A. 1974. *News and the Market*. Washington, D.C.: H. Regnery Co.

Koppel, Moshe/Shtrimberg, Itai. 2006. Good News or Bad News? Let the Market Decide. In *Computing Attitude and Affect in Text: Theory and Applications*. Dordrecht: Springer, 297–301.

Krishnamoorthy, Srikumar. 2017. Sentiment Analysis of Financial News Articles Using Performance Indicators. *Knowledge and Information Systems* 56, 1–22.

Kruskal, William H/Wallis, W Allen. 1952. Use of Ranks in One-Criterion Variance Analysis. *Journal of the American Statistical Association* 47/260, 583–621.

Kutuzov, Andrey/Øvrelid, Lilja/Szymanski, Terrence/Velldal, Erik. 2018. Diachronic Word Embeddings and Semantic Shifts: A Survey, 1384–97.

Labov, William. 1972. *Language in the Inner City: Studies in the Black English Vernacular*. Philadelphia: University of Pennsylvania Press.

Labov, William. 1984. Intensity. In Deborah Schiffrin (ed.). *Meaning and Use in Context*. Washington, D.C.: Georgetown University Press, 43–70.

Lau, Raymond YK/Li, Chunping/Liao, Stephen SY. 2014. Social Analytics: Learning Fuzzy Product Ontologies for Aspect-Oriented Sentiment Analysis. *Decision Support Systems* 65, 80–94.

Lemke, Jay L. 1998. Resources for Attitudinal Meaning: Evaluative Orientations in Text Semantics. *Functions of Language* 5/1, 33–56.

Li, Xiaodong et al. 2014. News Impact on Stock Price Return via Sentiment Analysis. *Knowledge-Based Systems* 69, 14–23.

Liu, Bing. 2010. Sentiment Analysis and Subjectivity. In Nitin Indurkhya /Fred J. Damerau (eds.). *Handbook of Natural Language Processing*. Oxfordshire: CRC Press, 627–66.

Liu, Bing. 2011. *Web Data Mining: Exploring Hyperlinks, Contents, and Usage Data*. Berlin: Springer.

Liu, Bing. 2012. *Sentiment Analysis and Opinion Mining*. San Rafael: Morgan & Claypool Publishers.

Liu, Bing. 2015. *Sentiment Analysis: Mining Opinions, Sentiments, and Emotions*. Cambridge: Cambridge University Press.

Liu, Yinhan et al. 2019. Roberta: A Robustly Optimized Bert Pretraining Approach. *arXiv preprint arXiv:1907.11692*.

Loughran, Tim/McDonald, Bill. 2011. When Is a Liability Not a Liability? Textual Analysis, Dictionaries, and 10-Ks. *The Journal of Finance* 66/1, 35–65.

Loughran, Tim/McDonald, Bill. 2015. The Use of Word Lists in Textual Analysis. *Journal of Behavioral Finance* 16/1, 1–11.

Loughran, Tim/McDonald, Bill. 2016. Textual Analysis in Accounting and Finance: A Survey. *Journal of Accounting Research* 54/4, 1187–1230.

Louw, Bill. 1993. Irony in the Text or Insincerity in the Writer? – The Diagnostic Potential of Semantic Prosodies. In Mona Baker et al. (eds.). *Text and Technology: In Honour of John Sinclair*. London: Longman, 240–51.

Luna-Alonso, Ana. 2016. La 'Refundación Del Capitalismo': Estudio Terminológico En La Prensa Francesa y Española. *Filologia e Linguística Portuguesa* 18/1, 145–74.

Lyons, John. 1977. *Semantics. Vol. 2*. Cambridge: Cambridge University Press.

Lyons, John. 1981. *Language and Linguistics: An Introduction*. Cambridge: Cambridge University Press.

Maas, Andrew L. et al. 2011. Learning Word Vectors for Sentiment Analysis. In *Proceedings of the 49th Annual Meeting of the Association for Computational Linguistics: Human Language Technologies*.

Malo, Pekka et al. 2014. Good Debt or Bad Debt: Detecting Semantic Orientations in Economic Texts. *Journal of the Association for Information Science and Technology* 65/4, 782–96.

Martin, John R./White, Peter R.R. 2005. *The Language of Evaluation: Appraisal in English*. Hampshire and New York: Palgrave Macmillan.

Martin, Katherin Connor. 2012. The Lexical Legacy of Occupy Wall Street. *Oxford Dictionaries Blog*. Available at https://web.archive.org/web/20170801055934/http://blog.oxforddictionaries.com/2012/09/occupy-wall-street/.

Massey, Doreen. 2013. Vocabularies of the Economy. *Soundings* 54/54, 9–22.

McEnery, Tony/Brezina, Vaclav/Baker, Helen. 2022. Usage Fluctuation Analysis: A New Way of Analysing Shifts in Historical Discourse. *International Journal of Corpus Linguistics*, 413–44.

McEnery, Tony/Xiao, Richard/Tono, Yukio. 2006. *Corpus-Based Language Studies: An Advanced Resource Book*. Taylor & Francis.

Melvin, Michael/Yin, Xixi. 2000. Public Information Arrival, Exchange Rate Volatility, and Quote Frequency. *The Economic Journal* 110/465, 644–61.

Mikolov, Tomas/Chen, Kai/Corrado, Greg/Dean, Jeffrey. 2013. Efficient Estimation of Word Representations in Vector Space.

arXiv:1301.3781 [cs]. Available at http://arxiv.org/abs/1301.3781 [Accessed on March 1, 2019].

Moessner, Lilo. 2003. *Diachronic English Linguistics: An Introduction*. Tübingen: Gunter Narr Verlag.

Mohammad, Saif M/Turney, Peter D. 2010. Emotions Evoked by Common Words and Phrases: Using Mechanical Turk to Create an Emotion Lexicon. In *Proceedings of the NAACL HLT 2010 Workshop on Computational Approaches to Analysis and Generation of Emotion in Text*. Association for Computational Linguistics, 26–34.

Mohammad, Saif/Dunne, Cody/Dorr, Bonnie. 2009. Generating High-Coverage Semantic Orientation Lexicons from Overtly Marked Words and a Thesaurus. In *Proceedings of the 2009 Conference on Empirical Methods in Natural Language Processing: Volume 2-Volume 2*. Association for Computational Linguistics, 599–608.

Mohammad, Saif/Kiritchenko, Svetlana/Zhu, Xiaodan. 2013. NRC-Canada: Building the State-of-the-Art in Sentiment Analysis of Tweets. In *Second Joint Conference on Lexical and Computational Semantics (* SEM), Volume 2: Proceedings of the Seventh International Workshop on Semantic Evaluation (SemEval 2013)*, 321–27.

Moirand, Sophie. 2007. *Les Discours de La Presse Quotidienne. Observer, Analyser, Comprendre*. Paris: Presses Universitaires de France.

Moirand, Sophie. 2016. 'La Construction de l'événement Dans La Presse Entre Sémantique Discursive, Hétérogénéités Énonciatives et Inscription de l'émotion'. Available at https://hal-univ-paris3.archives-ouvertes.fr/hal-01476098.

Montague, Richard. 1974. *Formal Philosophy: Selected Papers of Richard Montague. Ed. and with an Introd. by Richmond H. Thomason*. Yale University Press.

Moreno-Ortiz, Antonio. 2016. Lingmotif. Available at http://tecnolengua.uma.es/lingmotif.

Moreno-Ortiz, Antonio. 2017. Lingmotif: A user-focused sentiment analysis tool. *Procesamiento del Lenguaje Natural* 58, 133–40.

Moreno-Ortiz, Antonio/Fernández-Cruz, Javier. 2015. Identifying Polarity in Financial Texts for Sentiment Analysis: A Corpus-Based Approach. *Procedia – Social and Behavioral Sciences* 198, 330–38.

Moreno-Ortiz, Antonio/Fernandez-Cruz, Javier/Pérez-Hernández, Chantal. 2020. Design and Evaluation of SentiEcon: A Fine-Grained Economic/Financial Sentiment Lexicon from a Corpus of Business News. In *Proceedings of the 12th Language Resources and Evaluation Conference*. Marseille, France: European Language Resources Association, 5067–74. Available at https://www.aclweb.org/anthology/2020.lrec-1.623.

Moreno-Ortiz, Antonio/Pérez Pozo, Álvaro/Torres Sánchez, Sergio. 2010. Sentitext: Sistema de Análisis de Sentimiento Para El Español. *Procesamiento de Lenguaje Natural* 45, 297–98.

Moreno-Ortiz, Antonio/Pérez-Hernández, Chantal. 2014. Form and Function in Evaluative Language: The Use of Corpora to Identify Context Valence Shifters in a Linguistically-Motivated Sentiment Analysis System. In *The Functional Perspective on Language and Discourse*. Amsterdam: John Benjamins, 87–110.

Moreno-Ortiz, Antonio/Pérez-Hernandez, Chantal. 2018. Lingmotif-Lex: A Wide-Coverage, State-of-the-Art Lexicon for Sentiment Analysis. In *Proceedings of the Eleventh International Conference on Language Resources and Evaluation (LREC 2018)*. Miyazaki, Japan: European Language Resources Association (ELRA), 2653–59.

Moreno-Ortiz, Antonio/Pérez-Hernández, Chantal/Del-Olmo, María. 2013. Managing Multiword Expressions in a Lexicon-Based Sentiment Analysis System for Spanish. In *Proceedings of the 9th Workshop on Multiword Expressions MWE 2013*. Atlanta, USA: The Association for Computational Linguistics, 1–10. Available at https://www.aclweb.org/anthology/W/W13/W13-1000.pdf.

Moreno-Ortiz, Antonio/Pérez-Hernández, Chantal/Gómez-Pascual, Cristian. 2016. Extracting Domain-Specific Features for Sentiment Analysis Using Simple NLP Techniques: Running Shoes Reviews. In *EPiC Series in Language and Linguistics*. EasyChair, 298–307. Available at https://easychair.org/publications/paper/ppjg

Moreno-Ortiz, Antonio/Pineda Castillo, Francisco/Hidalgo García, Rodrigo. 2010. Análisis de Valoraciones de Usuario de Hoteles Con Sentitext: Un Sistema de Análisis de Sentimiento Independiente Del Dominio. *Procesamiento de Lenguaje Natural* 45, 31–39.

Musat, Claudiu/Trausan-Matu, Stefan. 2010. The Impact of Valence Shifters on Mining Implicit Economic Opinions. In *International Conference on Artificial Intelligence: Methodology, Systems, and Applications*. Springer, 131–40.

Neale, Bren/Flowerdew, Jennifer. 2003. Time, Texture and Childhood: The Contours of Longitudinal Qualitative Research. *International Journal of Social Research Methodology* 6/3, 189–99.

Niederhoffer, Victor. 1971. The Analysis of World Events and Stock Prices. *The Journal of Business* 44/2, 193–219.

Ochs, Elinor/Schieffelin, Bambi. 1989. Language Has a Heart. *Text-Interdisciplinary Journal for the Study of Discourse* 9/1, 7–26.

O'Hare, Neil et al. 2009. Topic-Dependent Sentiment Analysis of Financial Blogs. In *Proceedings of the 1st International CIKM Workshop on Topic-Sentiment Analysis for Mass Opinion*. ACM, 9–16.

Oliveira, Nuno/Cortez, Paulo/Areal, Nelson. 2016. Stock Market Sentiment Lexicon Acquisition Using Microblogging Data and Statistical Measures. *Decision Support Systems* 85, 62–73.

Osgood, Charles E/Richards, Meredith Martin. 1973. From Yang and Yin to and or But. *Language*, 380–412.

Oxford English Dictionary. 2019. Credit | Definition of Credit in English. *Oxford Dictionaries | English*. Available at https://en.oxforddictionaries.com/definition/credit [Accessed on February 9, 2019].

Pang, Bo/Lee, Lillian. 2005. Seeing Stars: Exploiting Class Relationships for Sentiment Categorization with Respect to Rating Scales. In *Proceedings of the 43rd Annual Meeting on Association for Computational Linguistics*. Association for Computational Linguistics, 115–24.

Pang, Bo/Lee, Lillian. 2008. Opinion Mining and Sentiment Analysis. *Foundations and Trends in Information Retrieval* 2/1–2, 1–135.

Pang, Bo/Lee, Lillian/Vaithyanathan, Shivakumar. 2002. Thumbs up?: Sentiment Classification Using Machine Learning Techniques. In *Proceedings of the ACL-02 Conference on Empirical Methods in Natural Language Processing – Volume 10*. Association for Computational Linguistics, 79–86. Available at http://portal.acm.org/citation.cfm?id=1118704&dl=GUIDE&coll=GUIDE&CFID=80308782&CFTOKEN=73139236

Partington, Alan. 2004. 'Utterly Content in Each Other's Company': Semantic Prosody and Semantic Preference. *International Journal of Corpus Linguistics* 9/1, 131–56.

Pedregosa, Fabian et al. 2011. Scikit-Learn: Machine Learning in Python. *Journal of Machine Learning Research* 12, 2825–30.

Pennebaker, James W/Boyd, Ryan L/Jordan, Kayla/Blackburn, Kate. 2015. *The Development and Psychometric Properties of LIWC2015*. Austin, USA: The University of Texas at Austin.

Perkins, Michael R. 1982. The Core Meanings of the English Modals. *Journal of Linguistics* 18/2, 245–73.

Pinedo, José María/Martínez, Ricardo. 2012. *Diccionario para entender la crisis y el rescate*. Córdoba: Editorial Almuzara.

Polanyi, Livia/Zaenen, Annie. 2006. Contextual Valence Shifters. In James G. Shanahan /Yan Qu /Janyce Wiebe (eds.). *Computing Attitude and Affect in Text: Theory and Applications*. Dordrecht: Springer, 1–10. Available at 10.1007/1-4020-4102-0_1.

Poon, Ser-Huang/Granger, Clive. 2005. Practical Issues in Forecasting Volatility. *Financial analysts journal* 61/1, 45–56.

Popescu, Ana-Maria/Etzioni, Oren. 2005. Extracting Product Features and Opinions from Reviews. In *Proceedings of the Conference on Human Language Technology and Empirical Methods in Natural Language Processing*. HLT '05: Association for Computational Linguistics, 339–46. Available at http://dx.doi.org/10.3115/1220 575.1220618

Price, Oliver/Mensio, Martino. 2022. Disagree. Available at https://git hub.com/o-P-o/disagree.

Provencio Garrigós, Herminia. 2016. Cambio semántico meliorativo de guapo: De la percepción olfativa y gustativa a la percepción visual. Available at http://rua.ua.es/dspace/handle/10045/61530

Riloff, Ellen/Wiebe, Janyce. 2003. Learning Extraction Patterns for Subjective Expressions. In *Proceedings of the 2003 Conference on Empirical Methods in Natural Language Processing*. EMNLP '03, Stroudsburg, USA: Association for Computational Linguistics, 105–12. Available at https://dl.acm.org/doi/10.3115/1119355.1119369

Rocci, Andrea/Palmieri, Rudi/Gautier, Laurent. 2015. Introduction to Thematic Section on Text and Discourse Analysis in Financial Communication. *Studies in Communication Sciences* 15/1, 2–4.

Rojo López, Ana María/Orts Llopis, María Ángeles. 2010. Metaphorical Pattern Analysis in Financial Texts: Framing the Crisis in Positive or Negative Metaphorical Terms. *Journal of Pragmatics* 42/12, 3300–13.

Salas-Zarate, María del Pilar et al. 2016. Sentiment Classification of Spanish Reviews: An Approach Based on Feature Selection and Machine Learning Methods. *J. UCS* 22/5, 691–708.

Sanh, Victor/Debut, Lysandre/Chaumond, Julien/Wolf, Thomas. 2019. DistilBERT, a Distilled Version of BERT: Smaller, Faster, Cheaper and Lighter. *ArXiv* abs/1910.01108.

Sarkozy, Nicolas. 2008. Speech by M. Nicolas Sarkozy, President of the Republic, to the European Parliament. Presented at the European Parliament, Strasbourg. Available at https://ca.ambafrance.org/Spe ech-by-M-Nicolas-Sarkozy [Accessed on June 20, 2023].

Saurí, Roser/Pustejovsky, James. 2009. FactBank: A Corpus Annotated with Event Factuality. *Language resources and evaluation* 43, 227–68.

Schumaker, Robert P./Chen, Hsinchun. 2009. Textual Analysis of Stock Market Prediction Using Breaking Financial News: The AZFin Text System. *ACM Transactions on Information Systems (TOIS)* 27/2, 12.

Shiller, Robert C. 2000. Irrational Exuberance. *Philosophy and Public Policy Quarterly* 20/1, 18–23.

Sinclair, J. 1991. *Corpus, Concordance, Collocation: Describing English Language.* Oxford: Oxford University Press.

Socher, Richard et al. 2013. Recursive Deep Models for Semantic Compositionality over a Sentiment Treebank. In *Proceedings of the 2013 Conference on Empirical Methods in Natural Language Processing.* Seattle, USA: Association for Computational Linguistics, 1631–42.

Srujan, K. S. et al. 2018. Classification of Amazon Book Reviews Based on Sentiment Analysis. In Vikrant Bhateja et al. (eds.). *Information Systems Design and Intelligent Applications.* Advances in Intelligent Systems and Computing. Singapore: Springer, 401–11.

Steward. Dominic. 2010. *Semantic Prosody: A Critical Evaluation.* New York: Routeledge.

Stone, Philip J./Hunt, Earl B. 1963. A Computer Approach to Content Analysis: Studies Using the General Inquirer System. In *Proceedings of the Spring Joint Computer Conference.* AFIPS '63 (Spring), New York, USA: ACM, 241–56. Available at http://doi. acm.org/10.1145/1461551.1461583

Stubbs, Michael. 1986. 'A Matter of Prolonged Field Work': Notes Towards a Modal Grammar of English. *Applied linguistics* 7/1, 1–25.

Stubbs, Michael. 2001. *Words and Phrases: Corpus Studies of Lexical Semantics.* Oxford: Blackwell.

Szarvas, György/Vincze, Veronika/Farkas, Richárd/Csirik, János. 2008. The BioScope Corpus: Annotation for Negation, Uncertainty and Their Scope in Biomedical Texts. In *Proceedings of the Workshop on Current Trends in Biomedical Natural Language Processing,* 38–45.

Taboada, Maite et al. 2011. Lexicon-Based Methods for Sentiment Analysis. *Computational linguistics* 37/2, 267–307.

Tao, Xiaohui/Zhou, Xujuan/Zhang, Ji/Yong, Jianming. 2016. Sentiment Analysis for Depression Detection on Social Networks. In *Advanced Data Mining and Applications.* Lecture Notes in Computer Science, Springer, Cham, 807–10. Available at https://link.springer.com/chapter/10.1007/978-3-319-49586-6_59

Temmerman, Rita. 2000. *Towards New Ways of Terminology Description: The Sociocognitive-Approach.* Amsterdam: John Benjamins Pub.

Tetlock, Paul C. 2007. Giving Content to Investor Sentiment: The Role of Media in the Stock Market. *The Journal of Finance* 62/3, 1139–68.

Tetlock, Paul C./Saar-Tsechansky, Maytal/Macskassy, Sofus. 2008. More than Words: Quantifying Language to Measure Firms' Fundamentals. *The Journal of Finance* 63/3, 1437–67.

Thompson, Geoff/Hunston, Susan. 2000. Evaluation: An Introduction. In Susan Hunston/Geoff Thompson (eds.). *Evaluation in Text: Authorial Stance and the Construction of Discourse.* Oxford: Oxford University Press, 1–26.

Toret Medina, Javier. 2015. *Tecnopolítica y 15M: La Potencia de Las Multitudes Conectadas. Un Estudio Sobre La Gestación y Explosión Del 15 M.* Barcelona: Editorial UOC.

Traugott, Elizabeth Closs. 1985. On Regularity in Semantic Change. *Journal of Literary Semantics* 14/3. Available at http://www.degruyter.com/view/j/jlse.1985.14.issue-3/jlse.1985.14.3.155/jlse.1985.14.3.155.xml

Traugott, Elizabeth Closs. 2000. Semantic Change: An Overview. In Lisa Cheng/Rint Sybesma (eds.). *The First Glot International State-of-the-Article Book*. Berlin: De Gruyter. Available at https://www.degruyter.com/document/doi/10.1515/9783110822861.385/html

Traugott, Elizabeth Closs/Dasher, Richard B. 2001. *Regularity in Semantic Change*. Cambridge: Cambridge University Press.

Trichet, Jean Claude/Papademos, Lucas. 2009. Introductory Statement with Q&A. Presented at the European Central Bank, Frankfurt-am-Main. Available at https://www.ecb.europa.eu/press/pressconf/2009/html/is090507.en.html [Accessed on June 24, 2023].

Tumitan, Diego/Becker, Karin. 2014. Sentiment-Based Features for Predicting Election Polls: A Case Study on the Brazilian Scenario. In *Proceedings of the 2014 IEEE/WIC/ACM International Joint Conferences on Web Intelligence (WI) and Intelligent Agent Technologies (IAT)-Volume 02*. IEEE Computer Society, 126–33.

Turney, Peter D. 2002. Thumbs Up or Thumbs Down? Semantic Orientation Applied to Unsupervised Classification of Reviews. In *Proceedings of the 40th Annual Meeting of the Association for Computational Linguistics (ACL)*. Philadelphia, 417–24. Available at https://aclanthology.org/P02-1053.pdf.

Van de Kauter, Marjan/Breesch, Diane/Hoste, Véronique. 2015. Fine-Grained Analysis of Explicit and Implicit Sentiment in Financial News Articles. *Expert Systems with applications* 42/11, 4999–5010.

Vincent, B. 2011. Biggest Cost of «Occupy Wall Street» Protests: Semantics. *The Examiner*. Available at http://www.examiner.com/article/biggest-cost-of-occupy-wall-street-protests-semantics

Waloszek, Aleksander/Waloszek, Wojciech. 2017. SACAM – A Model for Describing and Classifying Sentiment Analysis Methods: In *Proceedings of the 9th International Conference on Agents and Artificial Intelligence*. Porto, Portugal: SCITEPRESS – Science and Technology Publications, 196–206. Available at http://www.scitepress.org/DigitalLibrary/Link.aspx?doi=10.5220/0006199901960206 [Accessed on May 1, 2019].

Wang, Hao et al. 2012. A System for Real-Time Twitter Sentiment Analysis of 2012 US Presidential Election Cycle. In *Proceedings of the ACL 2012 System Demonstrations*. Association for Computational Linguistics, 115–20.

Whitsitt, Sam. 2005. A Critique of the Concept of Semantic Prosody. *International Journal of Corpus Linguistics* 10/3, 283–305.

Wiebe, Janyce. 2000. Learning Subjective Adjectives from Corpora. In *Proceedings of the 17th National Conference on Artificial Intelligence*. Menlo Park, CA: AAAI Press, 268–75. Available at http://www.aaai.org/Papers/AAAI/2000/AAAI00-113.pdf.

Wiebe, Janyce M/Bruce, Rebecca F/O'Hara, Thomas P. 1999. Development and Use of a Gold-Standard Data Set for Subjectivity Classifications. In *Proceedings of the 37th Annual Meeting of the Association for Computational Linguistics on Computational Linguistics*. Association for Computational Linguistics, 246–53.

Williams, Geoffrey. 2001. Mediating between Lexis and Texts: Collocational Networks in Specialised Corpora. *ASp* /31–33, 63–76.

Wilson, Theresa/Wiebe, Janyce/Hoffmann, Paul. 2005. Recognizing Contextual Polarity in Phrase-Level Sentiment Analysis. In *Proceedings of the Conference on Human Language Technology and Empirical Methods in Natural Language Processing*. HLT '05, Stroudsburg: Association for Computational Linguistics, 347–54. Available at http://dx.doi.org/10.3115/1220575.1220619.

Wood, Simon N. 2017. *Generalized Additive Models: An Introduction with R*. 2nd ed. Boca Ratón: Available at https://www.taylorfrancis.com/books/9781498728348

Yang, Zhilin et al. 2019. XLNet: Generalized Autoregressive Pretraining for Language Understanding. *Decision Support Systems* 55/4, 919–26.

Yu, Yang/Duan, Wenjing/Cao, Qing. 2013. The Impact of Social and Conventional Media on Firm Equity Value: A Sentiment Analysis Approach. *Decision Support Systems* 55/4, 919–26.

Zhang, Lei/Wang, Shuai/Liu, Bing. 2018. Deep Learning for Sentiment Analysis: A Survey. *Wiley Interdisciplinary Reviews: Data Mining and Knowledge Discovery* 8/4, e1253.

Zhang, Yongfeng et al. 2014. Explicit Factor Models for Explainable Recommendation Based on Phrase-Level Sentiment Analysis. In *Proceedings of the 37th International ACM SIGIR Conference on Research & Development in Information Retrieval*. ACM, 83–92.

Zhao, Zeyan/Ahmad, Khurshid. 2015. Qualitative and Quantitative Sentiment Proxies: Interaction Between Markets. In Konrad Jackowski et al. (eds.). *Intelligent Data Engineering and Automated*

Learning – IDEAL 2015. Cham: Springer International Publishing, 466–74. Available at http://link.springer.com/10.1007/978-3-319-24834-9_54.

Linguistic Insights

Studies in Language and Communication

This series aims to promote specialist language studies in the fields of linguistic theory and applied linguistics, by publishing volumes that focus on specific aspects of language use in one or several languages and provide valuable insights into language and communication research. A cross-disciplinary approach is favoured and most European languages are accepted.

The series includes two types of books:

- Monographs – featuring in-depth studies on special aspects of language theory, language analysis or language teaching.
- Collected papers – assembling papers from workshops, conferences or symposia.

Each volume of the series is subjected to a double peer-reviewing process.

Vol. 1   Maurizio Gotti & Marina Dossena (eds)
         Modality in Specialized Texts. Selected Papers of the 1st CERLIS Conference.
         421 pages. 2001. ISBN 3-906767-10-8 · US-ISBN 0-8204-5340-4

Vol. 2   Giuseppina Cortese & Philip Riley (eds)
         Domain-specific English. Textual Practices across Communities and Classrooms.
         420 pages. 2002. ISBN 3-906768-98-8 · US-ISBN 0-8204-5884-8

Vol. 3   Maurizio Gotti, Dorothee Heller & Marina Dossena (eds)
         Conflict and Negotiation in Specialized Texts. Selected Papers
         of the 2nd CERLIS Conference.
         470 pages. 2002. ISBN 3-906769-12-7 · US-ISBN 0-8204-5887-2

Vol. 4   Maurizio Gotti, Marina Dossena, Richard Dury, Roberta Facchinetti & Maria Lima
         Variation in Central Modals. A Repertoire of Forms and Types of Usage
         in Middle English and Early Modern English.
         364 pages. 2002. ISBN 3-906769-84-4 · US-ISBN 0-8204-5898-8

Editorial address:

Prof. Maurizio Gotti   Università di Bergamo, Dipartimento di Lingue, Letterature e Culture
                      Straniere Piazza Rosate 2, 24129 Bergamo, Italy
                      Fax: +39 035 2052789, E-Mail: m.gotti@unibg.it

Vol. 5   Stefania Nuccorini (ed.)
         Phrases and Phraseology. Data and Descriptions.
         187 pages. 2002. ISBN 3-906770-08-7 · US-ISBN 0-8204-5933-X

Vol. 6   Vijay Bhatia, Christopher N. Candlin & Maurizio Gotti (eds) Legal Discourse in Multilingual
         and Multicultural Contexts. Arbitration Texts in Europe.
         385 pages. 2003. ISBN 3-906770-85-0 · US-ISBN 0-8204-6254-3

Vol. 7   Marina Dossena & Charles Jones (eds) Insights into Late Modern English. 2nd edition. 378
         pages. 2003, 2007.
         ISBN 978-3-03911-257-9 · US-ISBN 978-0-8204-8927-8

Vol. 8   Maurizio Gotti
         Specialized Discourse. Linguistic Features and Changing Conventions. 351 pages. 2003,
         2005.
         ISBN 3-03910-606-6 · US-ISBN 0-8204-7000-7

Vol. 9   Alan Partington, John Morley & Louann Haarman (eds) Corpora and Discourse.
         420 pages. 2004. ISBN 3-03910-026-2 · US-ISBN 0-8204-6262-4

Vol. 10 Martina Möllering
         The Acquisition of German Modal Particles. A Corpus-Based Approach. 290 pages. 2004.
         ISBN 3-03910-043-2 · US-ISBN 0-8204-6273-X

Vol. 11 David Hart (ed.)
         English Modality in Context. Diachronic Perspectives.
         261 pages. 2003. ISBN 3-03910-046-7 · US-ISBN 0-8204-6852-5

Vol. 12 Wendy Swanson
         Modes of Co-reference as an Indicator of Genre.
         430 pages. 2003. ISBN 3-03910-052-1 · US-ISBN 0-8204-6855-X

Vol. 13 Gina Poncini
         Discursive Strategies in Multicultural Business Meetings. 2nd edition. 338 pages. 2004,
         2007.
         ISBN 978-3-03911-296-8 · US-ISBN 978-0-8204-8937-7

Vol. 14 Christopher N. Candlin & Maurizio Gotti (eds) Intercultural Aspects of Specialized Communication. 2nd edition. 369 pages. 2004, 2007.
         ISBN 978-3-03911-258-6 · US-ISBN 978-0-8204-8926-1

Vol. 15 Gabriella Del Lungo Camiciotti & Elena Tognini Bonelli (eds) Academic Discourse. New
         Insights into Evaluation.
         234 pages. 2004. ISBN 3-03910-353-9 · US-ISBN 0-8204-7016-3

Vol. 16 Marina Dossena & Roger Lass (eds)
         Methods and Data in English Historical Dialectology.
         405 pages. 2004. ISBN 3-03910-362-8 · US-ISBN 0-8204-7018-X

Vol. 17 Judy Noguchi
         The Science Review Article. An Opportune Genre in the Construction of Science.
         274 pages. 2006. ISBN 3-03910-426-8 · US-ISBN 0-8204-7034-1

Vol. 18 Giuseppina Cortese & Anna Duszak (eds)
         Identity, Community, Discourse. English in Intercultural Settings. 495 pages. 2005. ISBN
         3-03910-632-5 · US-ISBN 0-8204-7163-1

Vol. 19 Anna Trosborg & Poul Erik Flyvholm Jørgensen (eds) Business Discourse. Texts and Contexts.
         250 pages. 2005. ISBN 3-03910-606-6 · US-ISBN 0-8204-7000-7

Vol. 20   Christopher Williams
           Tradition and Change in Legal English. Verbal Constructions in Prescriptive Texts.
           2nd revised edition. 216 pages. 2005, 2007. ISBN 978-3-03911-444-3.

Vol. 21   Katarzyna Dziubalska-Kolaczyk & Joanna Przedlacka (eds) English Pronunciation Models:
           A Changing Scene.
           2nd edition. 476 pages. 2005, 2008. ISBN 978-3-03911-682-9.

Vol. 22   Christián Abello-Contesse, Rubén Chacón-Beltrán,
           M. Dolores López-Jiménez & M. Mar Torreblanca-López (eds) Age in L2 Acquisition and
           Teaching.
           214 pages. 2006. ISBN 3-03910-668-6 · US-ISBN 0-8204-7174-7

Vol. 23   Vijay K. Bhatia, Maurizio Gotti, Jan Engberg & Dorothee Heller (eds) Vagueness in Normative
           Texts.
           474 pages. 2005. ISBN 3-03910-653-8 · US-ISBN 0-8204-7169-0

Vol. 24   Paul Gillaerts & Maurizio Gotti (eds)
           Genre Variation in Business Letters. 2nd printing. 407 pages. 2008. ISBN 978-3-03911-
           681-2.

Vol. 25   Ana María Hornero, María José Luzón & Silvia Murillo (eds) Corpus Linguistics. Applications
           for the Study of English.
           2nd printing. 526 pages. 2006, 2008. ISBN 978-3-03911-726-0

Vol. 26   J. Lachlan Mackenzie & María de los Ángeles Gómez-González (eds) Studies in Functional
           Discourse Grammar.
           259 pages. 2005. ISBN 3-03910-696-1 · US-ISBN 0-8204-7558-0

Vol. 27   Debbie G. E. Ho
           Classroom Talk. Exploring the Sociocultural Structure of Formal ESL Learning. 2nd edi-
           tion. 254 pages. 2006, 2007. ISBN 978-3-03911-434-4

Vol. 28   Javier Pérez-Guerra, Dolores González-Álvarez, Jorge L. Bueno-Alonso & Esperanza Rama-
           Martínez (eds)
           'Of Varying Language and Opposing Creed'. New Insights into Late Modern English. 455
           pages. 2007. ISBN 978-3-03910-788-9

Vol. 29   Francesca Bargiela-Chiappini & Maurizio Gotti (eds) Asian Business Discourse(s).
           350 pages. 2005. ISBN 3-03910-804-2 · US-ISBN 0-8204-7574-2

Vol. 30   Nicholas Brownlees (ed.)
           News Discourse in Early Modern Britain. Selected Papers of CHINED 2004. 300 pages.
           2006. ISBN 3-03910-805-0 · US-ISBN 0-8204-8025-8

Vol. 31   Roberta Facchinetti & Matti Rissanen (eds) Corpus-based Studies of Diachronic English.
           300 pages. 2006. ISBN 3-03910-851-4 · US-ISBN 0-8204-8040-1

Vol. 32   Marina Dossena & Susan M. Fitzmaurice (eds)
           Business and Official Correspondence. Historical Investigations. 209 pages. 2006. ISBN 3-
           03910-880-8 · US-ISBN 0-8204-8352-4

Vol. 33   Giuliana Garzone & Srikant Sarangi (eds)
           Discourse, Ideology and Specialized Communication. 494 pages. 2007. ISBN 978-3-03910-
           888-6

Vol. 34   Giuliana Garzone & Cornelia Ilie (eds)
           The Use of English in Institutional and Business Settings. An Intercultural Perspective.
           372 pages. 2007. ISBN 978-3-03910-889-3

Vol. 35   Vijay K. Bhatia & Maurizio Gotti (eds) Explorations in Specialized Genres.
316 pages. 2006. ISBN 3-03910-995-2 · US-ISBN 0-8204-8372-9

Vol. 36   Heribert Picht (ed.)
Modern Approaches to Terminological Theories and Applications. 432 pages. 2006. ISBN 3-03911-156-6 · US-ISBN 0-8204-8380-X

Vol. 37   Anne Wagner & Sophie Cacciaguidi-Fahy (eds)
Legal Language and the Search for Clarity / Le langage juridique et la quête de clarté.
Practice and Tools / Pratiques et instruments.
487 pages. 2006. ISBN 3-03911-169-8 · US-ISBN 0-8204-8388-5

Vol. 38   Juan Carlos Palmer-Silveira, Miguel F. Ruiz-Garrido & Inmaculada Fortanet-Gómez (eds)
Intercultural and International Business Communication. Theory, Research and Teaching.
2nd edition. 343 pages. 2006, 2008. ISBN 978-3-03911-680-5

Vol. 39   Christiane Dalton-Puffer, Dieter Kastovsky, Nikolaus Ritt & Herbert Schendl (eds)
Syntax, Style and Grammatical Norms. English from 1500–2000. 250 pages. 2006. ISBN 3-03911-181-7 · US-ISBN 0-8204-8394-X

Vol. 40   Marina Dossena & Irma Taavitsainen (eds) Diachronic Perspectives on Domain-Specific English.
280 pages. 2006. ISBN 3-03910-176-0 · US-ISBN 0-8204-8391-5

Vol. 41   John Flowerdew & Maurizio Gotti (eds) Studies in Specialized Discourse.
293 pages. 2006. ISBN 3-03911-178-7

Vol. 42   Ken Hyland & Marina Bondi (eds) Academic Discourse Across Disciplines.
320 pages. 2006. ISBN 3-03911-183-3 · US-ISBN 0-8204-8396-6

Vol. 43   Paul Gillaerts & Philip Shaw (eds)
The Map and the Landscape. Norms and Practices in Genre. 256 pages. 2006. ISBN 3-03911-182-5 · US-ISBN 0-8204-8395-4

Vol. 44   Maurizio Gotti & Davide Giannoni (eds)
New Trends in Specialized Discourse Analysis.
301 pages. 2006. ISBN 3-03911-184-1 · US-ISBN 0-8204-8381-8

Vol. 45   Maurizio Gotti & Françoise Salager-Meyer (eds)
Advances in Medical Discourse Analysis. Oral and Written Contexts. 492 pages. 2006.
ISBN 3-03911-185-X · US-ISBN 0-8204-8382-6

Vol. 46   Maurizio Gotti & Susan Šarcevic´ (eds) Insights into Specialized Translation.
396 pages. 2006. ISBN 3-03911-186-8 · US-ISBN 0-8204-8383-4

Vol. 47   Khurshid Ahmad & Margaret Rogers (eds)
Evidence-based LSP. Translation, Text and Terminology. 584 pages. 2007. ISBN 978-3-03911-187-9

Vol. 48   Hao Sun & Dániel Z. Kádár (eds)
It's the Dragon's Turn. Chinese Institutional Discourses. 262 pages. 2008. ISBN 978-3-03911-175-6

Vol. 49   Cristina Suárez-Gómez
Relativization in Early English (950-1250). the Position of Relative Clauses. 149 pages.
2006. ISBN 3-03911-203-1 · US-ISBN 0-8204-8904-2

Vol. 50   Maria Vittoria Calvi & Luisa Chierichetti (eds) Nuevas tendencias en el discurso de especialidad. 319 pages. 2006. ISBN 978-3-03911-261-6

Vol. 51   Mari Carmen Campoy & María José Luzón (eds) Spoken Corpora in Applied Linguistics.
274 pages. 2008. ISBN 978-3-03911-275-3

Vol. 52   Konrad Ehlich & Dorothee Heller (Hrsg.) Die Wissenschaft und ihre Sprachen.
323 pages. 2006. ISBN 978-3-03911-272-2

Vol. 53   Jingyu Zhang
The Semantic Salience Hierarchy Model. The L2 Acquisition of Psych Predicates 273 pages.
2007. ISBN 978-3-03911-300-2

Vol. 54   Norman Fairclough, Giuseppina Cortese & Patrizia Ardizzone (eds) Discourse and Contemporary Social Change.
555 pages. 2007. ISBN 978-3-03911-276-0

Vol. 55   Jan Engberg, Marianne Grove Ditlevsen, Peter Kastberg & Martin Stegu (eds) New Directions in LSP Teaching.
331 pages. 2007. ISBN 978-3-03911-433-7

Vol. 56   Dorothee Heller & Konrad Ehlich (Hrsg.) Studien zur Rechtskommunikation.
322 pages. 2007. ISBN 978-3-03911-436-8

Vol. 57   Teruhiro Ishiguro & Kang-kwong Luke (eds) Grammar in Cross-Linguistic Perspective.
The Syntax, Semantics, and Pragmatics of Japanese and Chinese. 304 pages. 2012. ISBN 978-3-03911-445-0

Vol. 58   Carmen Frehner Email – SMS – MMS
294 pages. 2008. ISBN 978-3-03911-451-1

Vol. 59   Isabel Balteiro
The Directionality of Conversion in English. A Dia-Synchronic Study. 276 pages. 2007.
ISBN 978-3-03911-241-8

Vol. 60   Maria Milagros Del Saz Rubio
English Discourse Markers of Reformulation. 237 pages. 2007. ISBN 978-3-03911-196-1

Vol. 61   Sally Burgess & Pedro Martín-Martín (eds)
English as an Additional Language in Research Publication and Communication. 259 pages. 2008. ISBN 978-3-03911-462-7

Vol. 62   Sandrine Onillon
Pratiques et représentations de l'écrit.
458 pages. 2008. ISBN 978-3-03911-464-1

Vol. 63   Hugo Bowles & Paul Seedhouse (eds)
Conversation Analysis and Language for Specific Purposes. 2nd edition. 337 pages. 2007, 2009. ISBN 978-3-0343-0045-2

Vol. 64   Vijay K. Bhatia, Christopher N. Candlin & Paola Evangelisti Allori (eds) Language, Culture and the Law.
The Formulation of Legal Concepts across Systems and Cultures. 342 pages. 2008. ISBN 978-3-03911-470-2

Vol. 65   Jonathan Culpeper & Dániel Z. Kádár (eds) Historical (Im)politeness.
300 pages. 2010. ISBN 978-3-03911-496-2

Vol. 66   Linda Lombardo (ed.)
Using Corpora to Learn about Language and Discourse. 237 pages. 2009. ISBN 978-3-03911-522-8

Vol. 67 Natsumi Wakamoto
Extroversion/Introversion in Foreign Language Learning. Interactions with Learner Strategy Use.
159 pages. 2009. ISBN 978-3-03911-596-9

Vol. 68 Eva Alcón-Soler (ed.)
Learning How to Request in an Instructed Language Learning Context. 260 pages. 2008.
ISBN 978-3-03911-601-0

Vol. 69 Domenico Pezzini
The Translation of Religious Texts in the Middle Ages. 428 pages. 2008. ISBN 978-3-03911-600-3

Vol. 70 Tomoko Tode
Effects of Frequency in Classroom Second Language Learning. Quasi-experiment and stimulated-recall analysis.
195 pages. 2008. ISBN 978-3-03911-602-7

Vol. 71 Egor Tsedryk
Fusion symétrique et alternances ditransitives. 211 pages. 2009. ISBN 978-3-03911-609-6

Vol. 72 Cynthia J. Kellett Bidoli & Elana Ochse (eds) English in International Deaf Communication.
444 pages. 2008. ISBN 978-3-03911-610-2

Vol. 73 Joan C. Beal, Carmela Nocera & Massimo Sturiale (eds) Perspectives on Prescriptivism.
269 pages. 2008. ISBN 978-3-03911-632-4

Vol. 74 Carol Taylor Torsello, Katherine Ackerley & Erik Castello (eds) Corpora for University Language Teachers.
308 pages. 2008. ISBN 978-3-03911-639-3

Vol. 75 María Luisa Pérez Cañado (ed.)
English Language Teaching in the European Credit Transfer System. Facing the Challenge.
251 pages. 2009. ISBN 978-3-03911-654-6

Vol. 76 Marina Dossena & Ingrid Tieken-Boon van Ostade (eds)
Studies in Late Modern English Correspondence. Methodology and Data. 291 pages. 2008.
ISBN 978-3-03911-658-4

Vol. 77 Ingrid Tieken-Boon van Ostade & Wim van der Wurff (eds) Current Issues in Late Modern English.
436 pages. 2009. ISBN 978-3-03911-660-7

Vol. 78 Marta Navarro Coy (ed.)
Practical Approaches to Foreign Language Teaching and Learning. 297 pages. 2009. ISBN 978-3-03911-661-4

Vol. 79 Qing Ma
Second Language Vocabulary Acquisition. 333 pages. 2009. ISBN 978-3-03911-666-9

Vol. 80 Martin Solly, Michelangelo Conoscenti & Sandra Campagna (eds) Verbal/Visual Narrative Texts in Higher Education.
384 pages. 2008. ISBN 978-3-03911-672-0

Vol. 81 Meiko Matsumoto
From Simple Verbs to Periphrastic Expressions:
The Historical Development of Composite Predicates, Phrasal Verbs, and Related Constructions in English.
235 pages. 2008. ISBN 978-3-03911-675-1

Vol. 82   Melinda Dooly
         Doing Diversity. Teachers' Construction of Their Classroom Reality. 180 pages. 2009. ISBN 978-3-03911-687-4

Vol. 83   Victoria Guillén-Nieto, Carmen Marimón-Llorca & Chelo Vargas-Sierra (eds) Intercultural Business Communication and
         Simulation and Gaming Methodology. 392 pages. 2009. ISBN 978-3-03911-688-1

Vol. 84   Maria Grazia Guido
         English as a Lingua Franca in Cross-cultural Immigration Domains. 285 pages. 2008. ISBN 978-3-03911-689-8

Vol. 85   Erik Castello
         Text Complexity and Reading Comprehension Tests. 352 pages. 2008. ISBN 978-3-03911-717-8

Vol. 86   Maria-Lluisa Gea-Valor, Isabel García-Izquierdo & Maria-José Esteve (eds) Linguistic and Translation Studies in Scientific Communication.
         317 pages. 2010. ISBN 978-3-0343-0069-8

Vol. 87   Carmen Navarro, Rosa Ma Rodríguez Abella, Francesca Dalle Pezze & Renzo Miotti (eds)
         La comunicación especializada.
         355 pages. 2008. ISBN 978-3-03911-733-8

Vol. 88   Kiriko Sato
         The Development from Case-Forms to Prepositional Constructions in Old English Prose.
         231 pages. 2009. ISBN 978-3-03911-763-5

Vol. 89   Dorothee Heller (Hrsg.)
         Formulierungsmuster in deutscher und italienischer Fachkommunikation. Intra- und interlinguale Perspektiven.
         315 pages. 2008. ISBN 978-3-03911-778-9

Vol. 90   Henning Bergenholtz, Sandro Nielsen & Sven Tarp (eds) Lexicography at a Crossroads. Dictionaries and Encyclopedias Today, Lexicographical Tools Tomorrow.
         372 pages. 2009. ISBN 978-3-03911-799-4

Vol. 91   Manouchehr Moshtagh Khorasani
         The Development of Controversies. From the Early Modern Period to Online Discussion Forums.
         317 pages. 2009. ISBN 978-3-3911-711-6

Vol. 92   María Luisa Carrió-Pastor (ed.)
         Content and Language Integrated Learning. Cultural Diversity. 178 pages. 2009. ISBN 978-3-3911-818-2

Vol. 93   Roger Berry
         Terminology in English Language Teaching. Nature and Use. 262 pages. 2010. ISBN 978-3-0343-0013-1

Vol. 94   Roberto Cagliero & Jennifer Jenkins (eds) Discourses, Communities, and Global Englishes
         240 pages. 2010. ISBN 978-3-0343-0012-4

Vol. 95   Facchinetti Roberta, Crystal David, Seidlhofer Barbara (eds) From International to Local English – And Back Again.
         268 pages. 2010. ISBN 978-3-0343-0011-7

Vol. 96   Cesare Gagliardi & Alan Maley (eds)
         EIL, ELF, Global English. Teaching and Learning Issues 376 pages. 2010. ISBN 978-3-0343-0010-0

Vol. 97 Sylvie Hancil (ed.)
The Role of Prosody in Affective Speech. 403 pages. 2009. ISBN 978-3-03911-696-6

Vol. 98 Marina Dossena & Roger Lass (eds)
Studies in English and European Historical Dialectology. 257 pages. 2009. ISBN 978-3-0343-0024-7

Vol. 99 Christine Béal
Les interactions quotidiennes en français et en anglais.
De l'approche comparative à l'analyse des situations interculturelles. 424 pages. 2010. ISBN 978-3-0343-0027-8

Vol. 100 Maurizio Gotti (ed.)
Commonality and Individuality in Academic Discourse. 398 pages. 2009. ISBN 978-3-0343-0023-0

Vol. 101 Javier E. Díaz Vera & Rosario Caballero (eds)
Textual Healing. Studies in Medieval English Medical, Scientific and Technical Texts. 213 pages. 2009. ISBN 978-3-03911-822-9

Vol. 102 Nuria Edo Marzá
The Specialised Lexicographical Approach. A Step further in Dictionary-making. 316 pages. 2009. ISBN 978-3-0343-0043-8

Vol. 103 Carlos Prado-Alonso, Lidia Gómez-García, Iria Pastor-Gómez & David Tizón-Couto (eds)
New Trends and Methodologies in Applied English Language Research. Diachronic, Diatopic and Contrastive Studies.
348 pages. 2009. ISBN 978-3-0343-0046-9

Vol. 104 Françoise Salager-Meyer & Beverly A. Lewin Crossed Words. Criticism in Scholarly Writing? 371 pages. 2011. ISBN 978-3-0343-0049-0.

Vol. 105 Javier Ruano-García
Early Modern Northern English Lexis. A Literary Corpus-Based Study. 611 pages. 2010. ISBN 978-3-0343-0058-2

Vol. 106 Rafael Monroy-Casas
Systems for the Phonetic Transcription of English. Theory and Texts. 280 pages. 2011. ISBN 978-3-0343-0059-9

Vol. 107 Nicola T. Owtram
The Pragmatics of Academic Writing.
A Relevance Approach to the Analysis of Research Article Introductions. 311 pages. 2009. ISBN 978-3-0343-0060-5

Vol. 108 Yolanda Ruiz de Zarobe, Juan Manuel Sierra & Francisco Gallardo del Puerto (eds)
Content and Foreign Language Integrated Learning. Contributions to Multilingualism in European Contexts 343 pages. 2011. ISBN 978-3-0343-0074-2

Vol. 109 Ángeles Linde López & Rosalía Crespo Jiménez (eds)
Professional English in the European context. The EHEA challenge. 374 pages. 2010. ISBN 978-3-0343-0088-9

Vol. 110 Rosalía Rodríguez-Vázquez
The Rhythm of Speech, Verse and Vocal Music. A New Theory. 394 pages. 2010. ISBN 978-3-0343-0309-5

Vol. 111 Anastasios Tsangalidis & Roberta Facchinetti (eds) Studies on English Modality. In Honour of Frank Palmer. 392 pages. 2009. ISBN 978-3-0343-0310-1

Vol. 112	Jing Huang Autonomy, Agency and Identity in Foreign Language Learning and Teaching. 400 pages. 2013. ISBN 978-3-0343-0370-5
Vol. 113	Mihhail Lotman & Maria-Kristiina Lotman (eds) Frontiers in Comparative Prosody. In memoriam: Mikhail Gasparov. 426 pages. 2011. ISBN 978-3-0343-0373-6
Vol. 114	Merja Kytö, John Scahill & Harumi Tanabe (eds) Language Change and Variation from Old English to Late Modern English. A Festschrift for Minoji Akimoto 422 pages. 2010. ISBN 978-3-0343-0372-9
Vol. 115	Giuliana Garzone & Paola Catenaccio (eds) Identities across Media and Modes. Discursive Perspectives. 379 pages. 2009. ISBN 978-3-0343-0386-6
Vol. 116	Elena Landone Los marcadores del discurso y cortesía verbal en español. 390 pages. 2010. ISBN 978-3-0343-0413-9
Vol. 117	Maurizio Gotti & Christopher Williams (eds) Legal Discourse across Languages and Cultures. 339 pages. 2010. ISBN 978-3-0343-0425-2
Vol. 118	David Hirsh Academic Vocabulary in Context. 217 pages. 2010. ISBN 978-3-0343-0426-9
Vol. 119	Yvonne Dröschel Lingua Franca English. The Role of Simplification and Transfer. 358 pages. 2011. ISBN 978-3-0343-0432-0
Vol. 120	Tengku Sepora Tengku Mahadi, Helia Vaezian & Mahmoud Akbari Corpora in Translation. A Practical Guide. 135 pages. 2010. ISBN 978-3-0343-0434-4
Vol. 121	Davide Simone Giannoni & Celina Frade (eds) Researching Language and the Law. Textual Features and Translation Issues. 278 pages. 2010. ISBN 978-3-0343-0443-6
Vol. 122	Daniel Madrid & Stephen Hughes (eds) Studies in Bilingual Education. 472 pages. 2011. ISBN 978-3-0343-0474-0
Vol. 123	Vijay K. Bhatia, Christopher N. Candlin & Maurizio Gotti (eds) The Discourses of Dispute Resolution. 290 pages. 2010. ISBN 978-3-0343-0476-4
Vol. 124	Davide Simone Giannoni Mapping Academic Values in the Disciplines. A Corpus-Based Approach. 288 pages. 2010. ISBN 978-3-0343-0488-7
Vol. 125	Giuliana Garzone & James Archibald (eds) Discourse, Identities and Roles in Specialized Communication. 419 pages. 2010. ISBN 978-3-0343-0494-8
Vol. 126	Iria Pastor-Gómez The Status and Development of N+N Sequences in Contemporary English Noun Phrases. 216 pages. 2011. ISBN 978-3-0343-0534-1

Vol. 127   Carlos Prado-Alonso
Full-verb Inversion in Written and Spoken English. 261 pages. 2011. ISBN 978-3-0343-0535-8

Vol. 128   Tony Harris & María Moreno Jaén (eds) Corpus Linguistics in Language Teaching. 214 pages. 2010. ISBN 978-3-0343-0524-2

Vol. 129   Tetsuji Oda & Hiroyuki Eto (eds)
Multiple Perspectives on English Philology and History of Linguistics. A Festschrift for Shoichi Watanabe on his 80th Birthday.
378 pages. 2010. ISBN 978-3-0343-0480-1

Vol. 130   Luisa Chierichetti & Giovanni Garofalo (eds)
Lengua y Derecho. líneas de investigación interdisciplinaria. 283 pages. 2010. 978-3-0343-0463-4

Vol. 131   Paola Evangelisti Allori & Giuliana Garzone (eds)
Discourse, Identities and Genres in Corporate Communication. Sponsorship, Advertising and Organizational Communication. 324 pages. 2011. 978-3-0343-0591-4

Vol. 132   Leyre Ruiz de Zarobe & Yolanda Ruiz de Zarobe (eds) Speech Acts and Politeness across Languages and Cultures. 402 pages. 2012. 978-3-0343-0611-9

Vol. 133   Thomas Christiansen
Cohesion. A Discourse Perspective. 387 pages. 2011. 978-3-0343-0619-5

Vol. 134   Giuliana Garzone & Maurizio Gotti
Discourse, Communication and the Enterprise. Genres and Trends. 451 pages. 2011. ISBN 978-3-0343-0620-1

Vol. 135   Zsuzsa Hoffmann
Ways of the World's Words.
Language Contact in the Age of Globalization. 334 pages 2011. ISBN 978-3-0343-0673-7

Vol. 136   Cecilia Varcasia (ed.) Becoming Multilingual.
Language Learning and Language Policy between Attitudes and Identities. 213 pages. 2011. ISBN 978-3-0343-0687-5

Vol. 137   Susy Macqueen
The Emergence of Patterns in Second Language Writing. A Sociocognitive Exploration of Lexical Trails.
325 pages. 2012. ISBN 978-3-0343-1010-9

Vol. 138   Maria Vittoria Calvi & Giovanna Mapelli (eds)
La lengua del turismo. Géneros discursivos y terminología. 365 pages. 2011. ISBN 978-3-0343-1011-6

Vol. 139   Ken Lau
Learning to Become a Professional in a Textually-Mediated World. A Text-Oriented Study of Placement Practices.
261 pages. 2012. ISBN 978-3-0343-1016-1

Vol. 140   Sandra Campagna, Giuliana Garzone, Cornelia Ilie & Elizabeth Rowley-Jolivet (eds) Evolving Genres in Web-mediated Communication.
337 pages. 2012. ISBN 978-3-0343-1013-0

Vol. 141   Edith Esch & Martin Solly (eds)
The Sociolinguistics of Language Education in International Contexts. 263 pages. 2012.
ISBN 978-3-0343-1009-3

Vol. 142   Forthcoming.

Vol. 143   David Tizón-Couto
            Left Dislocation in English. A Functional-Discoursal Approach. 416 pages. 2012. ISBN 978-3-0343-1037-6

Vol. 144   Margrethe Petersen & Jan Engberg (eds)
            Current Trends in LSP Research. Aims and Methods. 323 pages. 2011. ISBN 978-3-0343-1054-3

Vol. 145   David Tizón-Couto, Beatriz Tizón-Couto, Iria Pastor-Gómez & Paula Rodríguez-Puente (eds) New Trends and Methodologies in Applied English Language Research II.
            Studies in Language Variation, Meaning and Learning. 283 pages. 2012. ISBN 978-3-0343-1061-1

Vol. 146   Rita Salvi & Hiromasa Tanaka (eds)
            Intercultural Interactions in Business and Management. 306 pages. 2011. ISBN 978-3-0343-1039-0

Vol. 147   Francesco Straniero Sergio & Caterina Falbo (eds) Breaking Ground in Corpus-based Interpreting Studies. 254 pages. 2012. ISBN 978-3-0343-1071-0

Vol. 148   Forthcoming.

Vol. 149   Vijay K. Bhatia & Paola Evangelisti Allori (eds)
            Discourse and Identity in the Professions. Legal, Corporate and Institutional Citizenship. 352 pages. 2011. ISBN 978-3-0343-1079-6

Vol. 150   Maurizio Gotti (ed.)
            Academic Identity Traits. A Corpus-Based Investigation. 363 pages. 2012. ISBN 978-3-0343-1141-0

Vol. 151   Priscilla Heynderickx, Sylvain Dieltjens, Geert Jacobs, Paul Gillaerts & Elizabeth de Groot (eds)
            The Language Factor in International Business.
            New Perspectives on Research, Teaching and Practice. 320 pages. 2012. ISBN 978-3-0343-1090-1

Vol. 152   Paul Gillaerts, Elizabeth de Groot, Sylvain Dieltjens, Priscilla Heynderickx & Geert Jacobs (eds)
            Researching Discourse in Business Genres. Cases and Corpora. 215 pages. 2012. ISBN 978-3-0343-1092-5

Vol. 153   Yongyan Zheng
            Dynamic Vocabulary Development in a Foreign Language. 262 pages. 2012. ISBN 978-3-0343-1106-9

Vol. 154   Carmen Argondizzo (ed.)
            Creativity and Innovation in Language Education. 357 pages. 2012. ISBN 978-3-0343-1080-2

Vol. 155   David Hirsh (ed.)
            Current Perspectives in Second Language Vocabulary Research. 180 pages. 2012. ISBN 978-3-0343-1108-3

Vol. 156   Seiji Shinkawa
            Unhistorical Gender Assignment in Lahamon's *Brut*. A Case Study of a Late Stage in the Development of Grammatical Gender toward its Ultimate Loss.
            186 pages. 2012. ISBN 978-3-0343-1124-3

Vol. 157   Yeonkwon Jung
Basics of Organizational Writing: A Critical Reading Approach. 151 pages. 2014. ISBN 978-3-0343-1137-3.

Vol. 158   Bárbara Eizaga Rebollar (ed.) Studies in Linguistics and Cognition.
301 pages. 2012. ISBN 978-3-0343-1138-0

Vol. 159   Giuliana Garzone, Paola Catenaccio, Chiara Degano (eds)
Genre Change in the Contemporary World. Short-term Diachronic Perspectives. 329 pages. 2012. ISBN 978-3-0343-1214-1

Vol. 160   Carol Berkenkotter, Vijay K. Bhatia & Maurizio Gotti (eds) Insights into Academic Genres. 468 pages. 2012. ISBN 978-3-0343-1211-0

Vol. 161   Beatriz Tizón-Couto
Clausal Complements in Native and Learner Spoken English. A corpus-based study with Lindsei and Vicolse. 357 pages. 2013. ISBN 978-3-0343-1184-7

Vol. 162   Patrizia Anesa
Jury Trials and the Popularization of Legal Language. A Discourse Analytical Approach. 247 pages. 2012. ISBN 978-3-0343-1231-8

Vol. 163   David Hirsh
Endangered Languages, Knowledge Systems and Belief Systems. 153 pages. 2013. ISBN 978-3-0343-1232-5

Vol. 164   Eugenia Sainz (ed.)
De la estructura de la frase al tejido del discurso. Estudios contrastivos español/italiano. 305 pages. 2014. ISBN 978-3-0343-1253-0

Vol. 165   Julia Bamford, Franca Poppi & Davide Mazzi (eds) Space, Place and the Discursive Construction of Identity. 367 pages. 2014. ISBN 978-3-0343-1249-3

Vol. 166   Rita Salvi & Janet Bowker (eds)
Space, Time and the Construction of Identity.
Discursive Indexicality in Cultural, Institutional and Professional Fields. 324 pages. 2013. ISBN 978-3-0343-1254-7

Vol. 167   Shunji Yamazaki & Robert Sigley (eds)
Approaching Language Variation through Corpora. A Festschrift in Honour of Toshio Saito. 421 pages. 2013. ISBN 978-3-0343-1264-6

Vol. 168   Franca Poppi
Global Interactions in English as a Lingua Franca. How written communication is changing under the influence of electronic media and new contexts of use.
249 pages. 2012. ISBN 978-3-0343-1276-9

Vol. 169   Miguel A. Aijón Oliva & María José Serrano
Style in syntax. Investigating variation in Spanish pronoun subjects. 239 pages. 2013. ISBN 978-3-0343-1244-8

Vol. 170   Inés Olza, Óscar Loureda & Manuel Casado-Velarde (eds)
Language Use in the Public Sphere. Methodological Perspectives and Empirical Applications 564 pages. 2014. ISBN 978-3-0343-1286-8

Vol. 171   Aleksandra Matulewska
Legilinguistic Translatology. A Parametric Approach to Legal Translation. 279 pages. 2013. ISBN 978-3-0343-1287-5

Vol. 172   Maurizio Gotti & Carmen Sancho Guinda (eds) Narratives in Academic and Professional Genres. 513 pages. 2013. ISBN 978-3-0343-1371-1

Vol. 173   Madalina Chitez
Learner corpus profiles. The case of Romanian Learner English. 244 pages. 2014. ISBN 978-3-0343-1410-7

Vol. 174   Chihiro Inoue
Task Equivalence in Speaking Tests.
251 pages. 2013. ISBN 978-3-0343-1417-6

Vol. 175   Gabriel Quiroz & Pedro Patiño (eds.)
LSP in Colombia: advances and challenges. 339 pages. 2014. ISBN 978-3-0343-1434-3

Vol. 176   Catherine Resche
Economic Terms and Beyond: Capitalising on the Wealth of Notions.
How Researchers in Specialised Varieties of English Can Benefit from Focusing on Terms.
332 pages. 2013. ISBN 978-3-0343-1435-0

Vol. 177   Wei Wang
Media representation of migrant workers in China. Identities and stances 198 pages. 2018. 978-3-0343-1436-7

Vol. 178   Cécile Desoutter & Caroline Mellet (dir.)
Le discours rapporté: approches linguistiques et perspectives didactiques. 270 pages. 2013. ISBN 978-3-0343-1292-9

Vol. 179   Ana Díaz-Negrillo & Francisco Javier Díaz-Pérez (eds) Specialisation and Variation in Language Corpora.
341 pages. 2014. ISBN 978-3-0343-1316-2

Vol. 180   Pilar Alonso
A Multi-dimensional Approach to Discourse Coherence. From Standardness to Creativity.
247 pages. 2014. ISBN 978-3-0343-1325-4

Vol. 181   Alejandro Alcaraz-Sintes & Salvador Valera-Hernández (eds) Diachrony and Synchrony in English Corpus Linguistics.
393 pages. 2014. ISBN 978-3-0343-1326-1

Vol. 182   Runhan Zhang
Investigating Linguistic Knowledge of a Second Language. 207 pages. 2015. ISBN 978-3-0343-1330-8

Vol. 183   Hajar Abdul Rahim & Shakila Abdul Manan (eds.) English in Malaysia. Postcolonial and Beyond.
267 pages. 2014. ISBN 978-3-0343-1341-4

Vol. 184   Virginie Fasel Lauzon
Comprendre et apprendre dans l'interaction. Les séquences d'explication en classe de français langue seconde.
292 pages. 2014. ISBN 978-3-0343-1451-0

Vol. 185   Forthcoming.

Vol. 186   Wei Ren
L2 Pragmatic Development in Study Abroad Contexts 256 pages. 2015. ISBN 978-3-0343-1358-2

Vol. 187 Marina Bondi & Rosa Lorés Sanz (eds)
Abstracts in Academic Discourse. Variation and Change. 361 pages. 2014. ISBN 978-3-0343-1483-1

Vol. 188 Giuditta Caliendo
Rethinking Community. Discourse, Identity and Citizenship in the European Union. 240 pages. 2017. ISBN 978-3-0343-1561-6

Vol. 189 Paola Evangelisti Allori (ed.) Identities in and across Cultures.
315 pages. 2014. ISBN 978-3-0343-1458-9

Vol. 190 Erik Castello, Katherine Ackerley & Francesca Coccetta (eds).
Studies in Learner Corpus Linguistics. Research and Applications for Foreign Language Teaching and Assessment.
358 pages. 2015. ISBN 978-3-0343-1506-7

Vol. 191 Ruth Breeze, Maurizio Gotti & Carmen Sancho Guinda (eds) Interpersonality in Legal Genres.
389 pages. 2014. ISBN 978-3-0343-1524-1

Vol. 192 Paola Evangelisti Allori, John Bateman & Vijay K. Bhatia (eds) Evolution in Genre. Emergence, Variation, Multimodality.
364 pages. 2014. ISBN 978-3-0343-1533-3

Vol. 193 Jiyeon Kook
Agency in Arzt-Patient-Gesprächen. Zur interaktionistischen Konzeptualisierung von Agency 271 pages. 2015. ISBN 978-3-0343-1666-8

Vol. 194 Susana Nicolás Román & Juan José Torres Núñez (eds)
Drama and CLIL. A new challenge for the teaching approaches in bilingual education. 170 pages. 2015. ISBN 978-3-0343-1629-3

Vol. 195 Alessandra Molino & Serenella Zanotti (eds)
Observing Norm, Observing Usage. Lexis in Dictionaries and in the Media. 430 pages. 2015. ISBN 978-3-0343-1584-5

Vol. 196 Begoña Soneira
A Lexical Description of English for Architecture. A Corpus-based Approach. 267 pages. 2015. ISBN 978-3-0343-1602-6

Vol. 197 M Luisa Roca-Varela
False Friends in Learner Corpora. A corpus-based study of English false friends in the written and spoken production of Spanish learners.
348 pages. 2015. ISBN 978-3-0343-1620-0

Vol. 198 Rahma Al-Mahrooqi & Christopher Denman
Bridging the Gap between Education and Employment. English Language Instruction in EFL Contexts.
416 pages. 2015. ISBN 978-3-0343-1681-1

Vol. 199 Rita Salvi & Janet Bowker (eds)
The Dissemination of Contemporary Knowledge in English. Genres, discourse strategies and professional practices.
171 pages. 2015. ISBN 978-3-0343-1679-8

Vol. 200 Maurizio Gotti & Davide S. Giannoni (eds)
Corpus Analysis for Descriptive and Pedagogical Purposes. ESP Perspectives. 432 pages. 2014. ISBN 978-3-0343-1516-6

Vol. 201   Ida Ruffolo
           The Perception of Nature in Travel Promotion Texts. A Corpus-based Discourse Analysis.
           148 pages. 2015. ISBN 978-3-0343-1521-0

Vol. 202   Ives Trevian
           English suffixes. Stress-assignment properties, productivity, selection and combinatorial processes.
           471 pages. 2015. ISBN 978-3-0343-1576-0

Vol. 203   Maurizio Gotti, Stefania Maci & Michele Sala (eds) Insights into Medical Communication.
           422 pages. 2015. ISBN 978-3-0343-1694-1

Vol. 204   Carmen Argondizzo (ed.)
           European Projects in University Language Centres. Creativity, Dynamics, Best Practice.
           371 pages. 2015. ISBN 978-3-0343-1696-5

Vol. 205   Aura Luz Duffé Montalván (ed.)
           Estudios sobre el léxico. Puntos y contrapuntos. 502 pages. 2016. ISBN 978-3-0343-2011-5

Vol. 206   Maria Pavesi, Maicol Formentelli & Elisa Ghia (eds)
           The Languages of Dubbing. Mainstream Audiovisual Translation in Italy. 275 pages. 2014.
           ISBN 978-3-0343-1646-0

Vol. 207   Ruth Breeze & Inés Olza (eds)
           Evaluation in media discourse. European perspectives. 268 pages. 2017. ISBN 978-3-0343-2014-6

Vol. 208   Vijay K. Bhatia & Maurizio Gotti (eds) Arbitration Discourse in Asia.
           331 pages. 2015. ISBN 978-3-0343-2032-0

Vol. 209   Sofía Bemposta-Rivas, Carla Bouzada-Jabois, Yolanda Fernández-Pena, Tamara Bouso, Yolanda J. Calvo-Benzies, Iván Tamaredo (eds)
           New trends and methodologies in applied English language research III. Synchronic and diachronic studies on discourse, lexis and grammar processing. 280 pages. 2017. ISBN 978-3-0343-2039-9

Vol. 210   Francisco Alonso Almeida, Laura Cruz García & Víctor González Ruiz (eds) Corpus-based studies on language varieties.
           285 pages. 2016. ISBN 978-3-0343-2044-3

Vol. 211   Juan Pedro Rica Peromingo
           Aspectos lingüísticos y técnicos de la traducción audiovisual (TAV). 177 pages. 2016. ISBN 978-3-0343-2055-9

Vol. 212   Maria Vender
           Disentangling Dyslexia. VenderPhonological and Processing Deficit in Developmental Dyslexia.
           338 pages. 2017. ISBN 978-3-0343-2064-1

Vol. 213   Zhilong Xie
           Bilingual Advantages. Contributions of Different Bilingual Experiences to Cognitive Control Differences Among Young-adult Bilinguals.
           221 pages. 2016. ISBN 978-3-0343-2081-8

Vol. 214   Larissa D'Angelo
           Academic posters. A textual and visual metadiscourse analysis. 367 pages. 2016. ISBN 978-3-0343-2083-2

Vol. 215 Evelyne Berger
Prendre la parole en L2. Regard sur la compétence d'interaction en classe de langue. 246 pages. 2016. ISBN 978-3-0343-2084-9

Vol. 216 David Lasagabaster and Aintzane Doiz (eds)
CLIL experiences in secondary and tertiary education: In search of good practices. 262 pages. 2016. ISBN 978-3-0343-2104-4

Vol. 217 Elena Kkese
Identifying Plosives in L2 English: The Case of L1 Cypriot Greek Speakers. 317 pages. 2016. ISBN 978-3-0343-2060-3

Vol. 218 Sandra Campagna, Elana Ochse, Virginia Pulcini & Martin Solly (eds)
Languaging in and across Communities: New Voices, New Identities. Studies in Honour of Giuseppina Cortese.
507 pages. 2016. ISBN 978-3-0343-2073-3

Vol. 219 Adriana Orlandi & Laura Giacomini (ed.)
Defining collocation for lexicographic purposes. From linguistic theory to lexicographic practice.
328 pages. 2016. ISBN 978-3-0343-2054-2

Vol. 220 Pietro Luigi Iaia
Analysing English as a Lingua Franca in Video Games. Linguistic Features, Experiential and Functional Dimensions of Online and Scripted Interactions. 139 pages. 2016. ISBN 978-3-0343-2138-9

Vol. 221 Dimitrinka G. Níkleva (ed.)
La formación de los docentes de español para inmigrantes en distintos contextos educativos. 390 pages. 2017. ISBN 978-3-0343-2135-8

Vol. 222 Katherine Ackerley, Marta Guarda & Francesca Helm (eds) Sharing Perspectives on English-Medium Instruction. 308 pages. 2017. ISBN 978-3-0343-2537-0

Vol. 223 Juana I. Marín-Arrese, Julia Lavid-López, Marta Carretero, Elena Domínguez Romero, Ma Victoria Martín de la Rosa & María Pérez Blanco (eds)
Evidentiality and Modality in European Languages. Discourse-pragmatic perspectives. 427 pages. 2017. ISBN 978-3-0343-2437-3

Vol. 224 Gilles Col
Construction du sens : un modèle instructionnel pour la sémantique. 292 pages. 2017. ISBN 978-3-0343-2572-1

Vol. 225 Ana Chiquito & Gabriel Quiroz (eds)
Pobreza, Lenguaje y Medios en América Latina. 362 pages. 2017. ISBN 978-3-0343-2142-6

Vol. 226 Xu Zhang
English Quasi-Numeral Classifiers. A Corpus-Based Cognitive-Typological Study. 360 pages. 2017. ISBN 978-3-0343-2818-0

Vol. 227 María Ángeles Orts, Ruth Breeze & Maurizio Gotti (eds)
Power, Persuasion and Manipulation in Specialised Genres. Providing Keys to the Rhetoric of Professional Communities.
368 pages. 2017. ISBN 978-3-0343-3010-7

Vol. 228 Maurizio Gotti, Stefania Maci & Michele Sala (eds)
Ways of Seeing, Ways of Being: Representing the Voices of Tourism. 453 pages. 2017. ISBN 978-3-0343-3031-2

Vol. 229　Dino Selvaggi
Plurilingual Code-Switching between Standard and Local Varieties. A Socio-Psycholinguistic Approach
371 pages. 2018. ISBN 978-3-0343-2663-6

Vol. 230　Anca-Cristina Sterie
Interprofessional interactions at the hospital. Nurses' requests and reports of problems in calls with physicians.
371 pages. 2017. ISBN 978-3-0343-2734-3

Vol. 231　Xiaodong Zhang
Understanding Chinese EFL Teachers' Beliefs and Practices in the Textbook-Based Classroom. 189 pages. 2017. ISBN 978-3-0343-3053-4

Vol. 232　Manuela Caterina Moroni & Federica Ricci Garotti (Hrsg.) Brücken schlagen zwischen Sprachwissenschaft und DaF-Didaktik. 345 pages. 2017. ISBN 978-3-0343-2667-4

Vol. 233　Dimitrinka Georgieva Níkleva
Necesidades y tendencias en la formación del profesorado de español como lengua extranjera
401 pages. 2017. ISBN 978-3-0343-2946-0

Vol. 234　Juan Santana-Lario & Salvador Valera (Hrsg.) Competing patterns in English affixation.
272 pages. 2017. ISBN 978-3-0343-2701-5

Vol. 235　Francisco Salgado-Robles
Desarrollo de la competencia sociolingüística por aprendices de español en un contexto de inmersión en el extranjero
241 pages. 2018. ISBN 978-3-0343-2323-9

Vol. 236　Maria Chiara Janner
Sguardi linguistici sulla marca. Analisi morfosintattica dei nomi commerciali in italiano
345 pages. 2017. ISBN 978-3-0343-2667-4

Vol. 237　Bárbara Herrero Muñoz-Cobo & Otman El Azami Zalachi La primavera del árabe marroquí.
192 pages. 2017. ISBN 978-3-0343-3104-3

Vol. 238　Consuelo Pascual Escagedo
El papel del oyente en la construcción de la conversación espontánea de estudiantes italianos en su interlengua y en su lengua materna
295 pages. 2017. ISBN 978-3-0343-3186-9

Vol. 239　Stefania M. Maci
The MS Digby 133 *Mary Magdalene*. Beyond scribal practices: language, discourse, values and attitudes.
336 pages. 2017. ISBN 978-3-0343-3256-9

Vol. 240　Eliecer Crespo-Fernández
Taboo in Discourse. Studies on Attenuation and Offence in Communication. 326 pages. 2018. ISBN 978-3-0343-3018-3

Vol. 241　Jana Altmanova, Maria Centrella, Katherine E. Russo (eds) Terminology & Discourse / Terminologie et discours.
424 pages. 2018. ISBN 978-3-0343-2417-5

Vol. 242　Xavier Blanco et Inès Sfar (dir.)
Lexicologie(s) : approches croisées en sémantique lexicale.
442 pages. 2018. ISBN 978-3-0343-3056-5

Vol. 243   Yunfeng Ge
            Resolution of Conflict of Interest in Chinese Civil Court Hearings. A Perspective of Discourse Information Theory.
            302 pages. 2018. ISBN 978-3-0343-3313-9

Vol. 244   Carla Vergaro
            Illocutionary Shell Nouns in English
            322 pages. 2018. ISBN 978-3-0343-3069-5

Vol. 245   Paolo Frassi
            L'adjectif en français et sa définition lexicographique. 270 pages. 2018. ISBN 978-3-0343-3394-8

Vol. 246   Suwilai Premsrirat and David Hirsh (eds) Language Revitalization. Insights from Thailand
            328 pages. 2018. ISBN 978-3-0343-3497-6

Vol. 247   Wei Wang
            Researching Learning and Learners in Genre-based Academic Writing Instruction 282 pages. 2018. ISBN 978-3-0343-3297-2

Vol. 248   Isusi Alabarte, Alberto & Lahuerta Martínez, Ana Cristina (eds) La comprensión lectora de lengua extranjera
            Estudio de los factores de familiaridad, interés, género y métodos de evaluación 336 pages. 2018. ISBN 978-3-0343-3493-8

Vol. 249   Mercedes Eurrutia Cavero
            Approche didactique du langage techno-scientifique Terminologie et discours
            374 pages. 2018. ISBN 978-3-0343-3512-6

Vol. 250   Aurora Ruiz Mezcua (ed.)
            Approaches to Telephone Interpretation Research, Innovation, Teaching and Transference
            268 pages. 2018. ISBN 978-3-0343-3330-6

Vol. 251   Morini Massimiliano A Day in the News
            A Stylistic Analysis of Newsspeak
            188 pages. 2018. ISBN 978-3-0343-3507-2

Vol. 252   Ignacio Guillén-Galve & Ignacio Vázquez-Orta (eds.)
            English as a Lingua Franca and Intercultural Communication Implications and Applications in the Field of English Language Teaching 414 pages. 2018. ISBN 978-3-0343-2763-3

Vol. 253   Bianca Del Villano
            Using the Devil with Courtesy
            Shakespeare and the Language of (Im)Politeness 216 pages. 2018. ISBN 978-3-0343-2315-4

Vol. 254   David Hirsh (ed.)
            Explorations in Second Language Vocabulary Research 252 pages. 2018. ISBN 978-3-0343-2940-8

Vol. 255   Tania Baumann (ed.)
            Reiseführer - Sprach- und Kulturmittlung im Tourismus / Le guide turistiche - mediazione linguistica e culturale in ambito turistico
            270 pages. 2018. ISBN 978-3-0343-3402-0

Vol. 256   Ariadna Sánchez-Hernández & Ana Herraiz-Martínez (eds) Learning second language pragmatics beyond traditional contexts 376 pages. 2018. ISBN 978-3-0343-3437-2

Vol. 257   Albert Bastardas-Boada, Emili Boix-Fuster, Rosa Maria Torrens (eds) Family Multilingualism in Medium-Sized Linguistic Communities 336 pages. 2019. ISBN 978-3-0343-2536-3

Vol. 258   Yuyang Cai
Examining the Interaction among Components of English for Specific Purposes Ability in Reading. The Triple-Decker Model
296 pages. 2020. 978-3-0343-2913-2

Vol. 259   Catia Nannoni
Participe présent et gérondif dans la presse française contemporaine 176 pages. 2019. ISBN 978-3-0343-3631-4

Vol. 260   Nieves Rodríguez Pérez & Bárbara Heinsch (eds.)
Contextos multilingües. Mediadores interculturales, formación del profesorado de lenguas extranjeras
289 pages. 2019. ISBN 978-3-0343-3768-7

Vol. 261   Giuliana Elena Garzone, Mara Logaldo, Francesca Santulli (eds.) Investigating Conflict Discourses in the Periodical Press
244 pages. 2020. ISBN 978-3-0343-3668-0

Vol. 262   Laura Nadal
Lingüística experimental y contraargumentación 233 pages. 2019. ISBN 978-3-0343-3791-5

Vol. 263   Claudia Claridge & Merja Kytö (eds.)
Punctuation in Context – Past and Present Perspectives 288 pages. 2019. ISBN 978-3-0343-3790-8

Vol. 264   Maurizio Gotti, Stefania Maci, Michele Sala (eds.) Scholarly Pathways
530 pages. 2020. ISBN 978-3-0343-3860-8

Vol. 265   Ruth Breeze, Ana M. Fernández Vallejo (eds.) Politics and populism across modes and media
350 pages. 2020. ISBN 978-3-0343-3707-6

Vol. 266   Jean Marguerite Jimenez
Understanding the Effects of Immediate Electronic Corrective Feedback on Second Language Development
252 pages. 2020. ISBN 978-3-0343-3815-8

Vol. 267   Sergio Rodríguez-Tapia, Adela González-Fernández (eds)
Lenguas y turismo: estudios en torno al discurso, la didáctica y la divulgación 380 pages. 2020. ISBN 978-3-0343-3881-3

Vol. 268   Ana Bocanegra-Valle (ed.)
Applied Linguistics and Knowledge Transfer. Employability, Internationalisation and Social Challenges
344 pages. 2020. ISBN 978-3-0343-3714-4

Vol. 269   Beatrice Garzelli
La traducción audiovisual español-italiano.Películas y cortos entre humor y habla soez 202 pages. 2020. ISBN 978-3-0343-4013-7

Vol. 270   Iván Tamaredo
Complexity, Efficiency, and Language Contact. Pronoun Omission in World Englishes 292 pages. 2020. ISBN 978-3-0343-3902-5

Vol. 271   Silvia Domenica Zollo,
Origine et histoire du vocabulaire des arts de la table. Analyse lexicale et exploitation de corpus textuels
239 pages. 2020. ISBN 978-3-0343-3890-5

Vol. 272　Paola Paissa, Michelangelo Conoscenti, Ruggero Druetta, Martin Solly (eds.) Metaphor and Conflict / Métaphore et conflit
385 pages. 2021. 978-3-0343-4068-7

Vol. 273　María Martínez-Atienza de Dios,
Entre el léxico y la sintaxis: las fases de los eventos 178 pages. 2021. 978-3-0343-4173-8

Vol. 274　Noelia Castro-Chao,
Argument Structure in Flux. The Development of Impersonal Constructions in Middle and Early Modern English, with Special Reference to Verbs of Desire.
300 pages. 2021. 978-3-0343-4189-9

Vol. 275　Gabriella Carobbio, Cécile Desoutter, Aurora Fragonara (eds.)
Macht, Ratio und Emotion: Diskurse im digitalen Zeitalter / Pouvoir, raison et émotion: les discours à l'ère du numérique
246 pages. 2020. 978-3-0343-4184-4

Vol. 276　Miguel Fuster-Márquez, José Santaemilia, Carmen Gregori-Signes, Paula Rodríguez-Abruñeiras (eds.)
Exploring discourse and ideology through corpora 293 pages. 2021. 978-3-0343-3969-8

Vol. 277　Tamara Bouso
Changes in Argument Structure
The Transitivizing Reaction Object Construction
392. 2021. 978-3-0343-4095-3

Vol. 278　Maria Luisa Maggioni, Amanda Murphy (eds.) Back to the Future. English from Past to Present 250 pages. 2021. 978-3-0343-4273-5

Vol. 279　Luisa Chierichetti
Diálogos de serie. Una aproximación a la construcción discursiva de personajes basada en corpus
246 pages. 2021. 978-3-0343-4274-2

Vol. 280　Cristina Lastres-López
From subordination to insubordination. A functional-pragmatic approach to if/si-constructions in English, French and Spanish spoken discourse
258 pages. 2021. 978-3-0343-4220-9

Vol. 281　Eleonora Federici, Stefania Maci (eds.)
Gender issues. Translating and mediating languages, cultures and societies 500 pages. 2021. 978-3-0343-4022-9

Vol. 282　José Mateo, Francisco Yus (eds.)
Metaphor in Economics and specialised Discourse 354 pages. 2021. 978-3-0343-4048-9

Vol. 283　Nicholas Brownlees (ed.)
The Role of Context in the Production and Reception of Historical News Discourse 376 pages. 2021. 978-3-0343-4181-3

Vol. 284　Catalina Fuentes Rodriguez, María Ester Brenes Peña, Víctor Pérez Béjar (eds.) Sintaxis discursiva: construcciones y operadores en español
396 pages. 2021. 978-3-0343-4306-0

Vol. 285　Dominic Stewart
Frequency in the dictionary. A corpus-assisted contrastive analysis of English and Italian
176 pages. 2021. 978-3-0343-4368-8

Vol. 286   Carla Bouzada-Jabois
Nonfinite supplements in the recent history of English 320 pages. 2021. 978-3-0343-4226-1

Vol. 287   Sofía Bemposta Rivas
Verb-governed infinitival complementation in the recent history of English 320 pages. 2021. 978-3-0343-4227-8

Vol. 288   Mirella Agorni
Translating Italy for the Nineteenth Century. Translators and an Imagined Nation in the Early Romantic Period 1816–1830s
180 pages. 2021. 978-3-0343-3612-3

Vol. 289   David Hirsh (ed.)
Research Perspectives in Language and Education 276 pages. 2021. 978-3-0343-4219-3

Vol. 290   Federica Vezzani
Terminologie numérique : conception, représentation et gestion 238 pages. 2022. 978-3-0343-4394-7

Vol. 291   Stefania M. Maci
Evidential verbs in the genre of medical posters. A corpus-based analysis 498 pages. 2022. 978-3-0343-4521-7

Vol. 292   Francisco J. Álvarez-Gil
Stance devices in tourism-related research articles: A corpus-based study 170 pages. 2022. 978-3-0343-4555-2

Vol. 293   Annalisa Baicchi / Stefania Biscetti (eds.)
The Language of Fashion. Linguistic, Cognitive, and Cultural Insights
190 pages. 2022. 978-3-0343-4428-9

Vol. 294   Ana Maria Piquer-Píriz
E-learning in EMI. Academic language for university students
200 pages. 2022. 978-3-0343-4589-7

Vol. 295   Geneviève Henrot Sostero (ed.)
Alle radici della fraseologia europea
400 pages. 2023. 978-3-0343-4645-0

Vol. 296   Klara Dankova
Les fibres textiles entre synchronie et diachronie: études terminologiques 300 pages. 2023. 978-3-0343-4587-3

Vol. 297   Marta Carretero, Juana I. Marín-Arrese, Elena Domínguez Romero, Mª Victoria Martín de la Rosa (eds.) Evidentiality and Epistemic Modality. Conceptual and Descriptive issues
350 pages. 2023. 978-3-0343-3993-3

Vol. 298   Kim Grego, Alessandra Vicentini, Virpi Ylänne (eds.) Age-Specific Issues. Language, Spaces, Technologies
300 pages. 2023. 978-3-0343-4411-1

Vol. 299   Giovanni Garofalo (ed.) Estudios de género asistidos por corpus.
Enfoques multidisciplinarios
292 pages. 2022. 978-3-0343-4548-4

Vol. 300   Giuseppe Palumbo, Katia Peruzzo, Gianluca Pontrandolfo (eds.)
What's Special About Specialised Translation? Essays in Honour of Federica Scarpa
296 pages. 2023. 978-3-0343-4411-1

Vol. 301 Raquel P. Romasanta
Probabilistic variability in clausal verb complementation in World Englishes.
390 pages. 2023. 978-3-0343-4703-7

Vol. 302 Giulia Adriana Pennisi
A linguistic Insight into Legislative Drafting. Tradition and Change in the UK Legislation
330 pages. 2023. 978-3-0343-4700-6

Vol. 303 Javier Fernández-Cruz, Antonio Moreno-Ortiz
Economic terms in the news during the Great Recession. A diachronic sentiment and collocational analysis
193 pages. 2024. 978-3-0343-4778-5

Printed in the USA
CPSIA information can be obtained
at www.ICGtesting.com
LVHW041825041124
795688LV00002B/159